Alcohol in World H

From the origins of drinking to the use and abuse of alcohol in the present day, this global historical study draws on approaches and research from biology, anthropology, sociology, and psychology. Topics covered include:

- the impact of colonialism
- alcohol before the world economy
- industrialization and alcohol
- globalization, consumer society, and alcohol.

Gina Hames argues that the production, trade, consumption, and regulation of alcohol have shaped virtually every civilization in numerous ways. It has perpetuated the development of both domestic and international trade; helped create identity and define religion; provided a tool for oppression as well as a tool for cultural and political resistance; and has supplied governments with essential revenues as well as a means of control over minority groups.

Alcohol in World History is one of the first studies to pull together such a wide range of sources in order to compare the role of alcohol throughout time and across both Western and non-Western civilizations.

Gina Hames is an assistant professor at Pacific Lutheran University. Her research interests include alcohol and the creation of identity in early twentieth-century Bolivia and in the late twentieth- and early twenty-first-century United States.

Themes in World History
Series editor: Peter N. Stearns

The *Themes in World History* series offers focused treatment of a range of human experiences and institutions in the world history context. The purpose is to provide serious, if brief, discussions of important topics as additions to textbook coverage and document collections. The treatments will allow students to probe particular facets of the human story in greater depth than textbook coverage allows, and to gain a fuller sense of historians' analytical methods and debates in the process. Each topic is handled over time – allowing discussions of changes and continuities. Each topic is assessed in terms of a range of different societies and religions – allowing comparisons of relevant similarities and differences. Each book in the series helps readers deal with world history in action, evaluating global contexts as they work through some of the key components of human society and human life.

Alcohol in World History

Gina Hames

Routledge
Taylor & Francis Group

LONDON AND NEW YORK

First published 2012
by Routledge
2 Park Square, Milton Park, Abingdon, Oxon OX14 4RN

Simultaneously published in the USA and Canada
by Routledge
711 Third Avenue, New York, NY 10017

Routledge is an imprint of the Taylor & Francis Group, an informa business

British Library Cataloguing in Publication Data
A catalogue record for this book is available from the British Library

Library of Congress Cataloging in Publication Data
Hames, Gina.
 Alcohol in world history / Gina Hames.
  p. cm. – (Themes in world history)
 Includes bibliographical references.
 1. Drinking of alcoholic beverages–History. 2. Alcoholic beverages–Social
aspects–History. 3. Alcoholic beverage industry–Social aspects–History. I.
Title.
 HV5020.H36 2012
 394.1'309–dc23
                2011044427

ISBN: 978-0-415-31151-9 (hbk)
ISBN: 978-0-415-31152-6 (pbk)
ISBN: 978-0-203-46305-5 (ebk)

Typeset in Times New Roman
by Taylor & Francis Books

Contents

Acknowledgements

I especially thank Peter N. Stearns for his continued support. I also thank the editors at Routledge who have been very helpful to me throughout this project. Finally, I would like to thank my very talented student research assistants, Margaret Cox, Samm Thompson, Breanne Compton, Luke Dolge, and Ronan Rooney who assisted me during the beginning stages of the research.

Introduction

Alcohol has influenced virtually every civilization. Alcohol production, trade, consumption, and regulation have helped shape the cultural, social, political, and economic spheres in societies around the world. Consumption of alcohol began when humans discovered natural fermentation as hunter-gatherers. When people settled into agricultural societies, one of the first substances they produced was alcohol. Moreover, alcohol was one of the first commodities traded among groups. Alcohol has been central in the most important social and cultural ceremonies, especially rites of passage such as births, funerals, initiations, and marriages. It has also been a vital part of feasts, magic rites, worship, and hospitality.

Alcohol has provided people in many cultures with essential, daily nourishment, as well as safe fluids to drink where water remained contaminated. Alcohol has shaped traditional medicinal remedies in most cultures and has continued to be used in that way into the twenty-first-century. The meanings and uses of alcohol have affected gender roles, class stratification, social hierarchies, and ethnic identities. Governments have capitalized on the popularity of alcohol, regulating its production, sale, and consumption to gain power and money. And economies have flourished because of its trade. In fact, many have argued that alcohol has been the most significant form of material culture in the lives of the world's peoples.

Academic disciplines study alcohol

Each academic discipline has approached the study of alcohol differently. Chemists have been interested in the chemical processes of the fermentation of alcohol, meaning what happens at the molecular level. Economists have studied the market for alcohol. They have been interested in the factors that have led to the amount of alcohol purchased and the amount produced and sold. Anthropologists have concentrated on the meanings of alcohol in cultural and social rituals, and sociologists have focused on alcohol use in social activities. People's behavioral reactions to alcohol have been studied by social scientists, including sociologists, anthropologists, and psychologists. The regulation of alcohol has been studied by political scientists, who have focused on the individual and structural constraints surrounding alcohol. Finally, historians have been interested in the role of alcohol across civilizations, the change or continuity in that role over time, and the causes of those changes or continuities.

Several disciplines have focused on the abuse and disease aspects of alcohol. Sociologists and psychologists have studied the disease and treatment of alcoholism. Sociologists, psychologists, and social workers have studied alcohol abuse. Sociologists have analyzed how alcohol has been defined as a disease as well as the social indicators that have caused the disease, such as family background, gender, and class. They have also wanted to know the prevalence of the disease in society. Psychologists have questioned the etiology of the abuse of alcohol, in other words the neuro-chemical, behavioral, and genetic origins of the abuse of alcohol. Moreover, they have studied the prevention of abuse as well as treatment of abuse through behavioral, pharmacological, and social support means. In the hard sciences, chemists have analyzed the chemical process of alcohol metabolism in the body as well as the long-term chemical and physical effects of alcohol on certain organs of the body, like the brain, heart, kidneys, and liver. They have also asked questions about the biochemical basis of alcohol addiction. Biologists have also sought to pinpoint the physical effects of alcohol, especially the effects of abuse. They have tested insects, animals, and humans in order to find out how alcohol is metabolized.

This work uses both the natural and social sciences in a global context to understand more fully alcohol in world history. One way to begin to synthesize the links between the bio-chemical, socio-psychological, and cultural–historical approaches to alcohol studies is to compare alcohol production, trade, consumption, and regulation across cultures and through time. Human interactions during these processes highlight themes such as religious rituals, gender relations, class structures, ethnic identities, political structures, and economic systems, all of which help to understand world history.

What is alcohol?

The word alcohol originated in Arabic. A popular theory contends that it comes from the word al-kuhul. According to this theory, the meaning of al-kuhul was first used to describe distilled substances in general, and then narrowed to mean specifically ethanol. By 1672 this conjectured etymology began circulating in Britain, and now can be found in many dictionaries. There are three kinds of alcoholic beverages: wine, beer, and spirits. Wines are fermented from the sap of plants, honey, milk, and fruits or berries, especially grapes. Beers are fermented from grains such as wheat, corn, hops, and barley. Spirits are distilled from beer, wine, or other substances. The main ingredient that provides the effect of all these beverages is ethyl alcohol, or ethanol.

Alcoholic beverages contain more than ethyl alcohol, however. They contain secondary ingredients such as acids, aldehydes, ketones, phenols, tannins, vitamins, and minerals. Alcohol content varies by product. Commercially produced beer contains between 2 and 8 percent alcohol; wine contains between 8 and 14 percent alcohol; fortified wines, such as port, contain between 20 and 21 percent alcohol; and spirits such as vodka and gin contain between 40 and 50 percent alcohol. Traditionally made alcoholic beverages, such as corn beer, or *chicha*, in the Andes, fermented maguey juice, or *pulque*, in Mexico, palm wine and banana beer in parts of Africa, and *kumiss*, made from mare's milk in Mongolia, can contain anywhere from less than 1 percent alcohol up to 4 percent, depending upon the individual maker. Furthermore, there are nutritional differences between beer and wine. For example, in the nutritional comparison between one drink of wine, about 3 ½ ounces, and one drink of beer, about 12 ounces, beer wins with almost twice as much energy as wine. In fact, the food value of strong beers such as lager is similar to that of milk, but milk contains much more fat and cholesterol.

Outline of the book

The book is divided into seven chapters. Each chapter explores, in some combination, the production, trade, consumption, and regulation of alcohol across cultures and within cultures in a particular time period. First, the production and trade of alcohol are viewed through an economic as well as socio-cultural lens. Second, the consumption of alcohol, which includes nutritional, medicinal, social, and ritual uses of alcohol, are examined through a biological, anthropological, and sociological lens. Third, the regulation of alcohol is studied from political, sociological, and anthropological perspectives. Finally, all of these aspects of alcohol are analyzed historically. Historical questions include: Is there more change or continuity over time? Are there more differences or similarities across civilizations within the same time period? And what are the results of global contacts among civilizations over time?

Chapters 1, 2, and 3 examine alcohol in pre-modern world history, up to roughly 1450. The first chapter explains the origins of alcohol using archaeological evidence. It examines the kinds of alcohol, their contents, and their processes of production as well as alcohol's influence on the development of ancient Egypt, Mesopotamia (including Jewish society), China, India, and the Americas. Chapter 2 concentrates on the Classical period. It examines alcohol in the classical societies of Greece and Rome, China, and India, studying especially the uses of alcohol for nutrition and rituals, as well as how alcohol was used to signify social hierarchies. Chapter 3 moves on to the Post-Classical era in the Middle East, the isolated Aztec and Inca empires, medieval Eastern and Western Europe, and Japan, focusing on the spread of culture in the Middle East, the social and cultural meanings of production and use in the Americas, Eastern Europe, and Japan, and the modernization of trade in the West.

Chapters 4 through 7 explain the role of alcohol in societies from roughly 1450 up to the beginning of the twenty-first-century. Chapter 4 first analyzes the role of alcohol in the world economic system, using the perspective of the

West. It then explains the significance of alcohol in the Atlantic slave trade
and the subsequent influence of alcohol in Africa. Next, it focuses on colonial
contact in Latin America and North America, especially religious contact
and its influence on drinking patterns. Last it analyzes the political agendas
behind the regulation of alcohol by the colonial governments.

Chapter 5 discusses the uses and regulations of alcohol during industrialization, focusing on the Western countries of Britain, Ireland, France, and
the United States, as well as the non-Western countries of Japan and Russia.
It also compares the temperance movements across these societies. Chapter 6
examines the second great wave of colonialism in Africa, India, and Australia. It
investigates how colonialism changed drinking patterns in all of these areas,
as well as how the colonized used alcohol to maintain their traditions in the
face of change. Chapter 7 covers the twentieth-century and the beginnings of
the twenty-first-centuries, concentrating on the functions of alcohol in the
process of cultural and economic globalization, especially the infiltration of
Western culture into non-Western societies. The chapter uses Latin America,
Africa, Saudi Arabia, India, China, Japan, Russia, France, and the United States
to illustrate these trends.

The book pays particular attention to the following issues: (1) the significance of place and agriculture for the creation of alcohol; (2) the meanings
of alcohol use in cultural construction; (3) the ritual significance of alcohol;
(4) the beliefs about alcohol that reinforce patriarchy and, alternatively, those
that empower women; (5) the role of alcohol in supporting existing social
hierarchies or conversely upsetting the status quo; (6) alcohol culture as a
means for Westernization or on the contrary as a tool to resist Westernization;
(7) the uses of alcohol by governments; and (8) the significance of alcohol as a
commodity.

1 The origins of alcohol

Between 8000 and 3500 BCE, sometimes called the Neolithic Age, or the new Stone Age, humans made one of the biggest shifts in human history; they moved from hunting and gathering to agricultural production. The development of stable, permanent agricultural societies occurred over a period of thousands of years. The rise of agriculture meant that larger groups of people could live within a prescribed area, because agriculture could support more people per parcel of land than could hunting and gathering. These concentrated groups invented better tools and began writing for the first time, which led to a higher degree of social complexity.

Many authors argue that in addition to tools and writing, the use of alcohol in emerging civilizations represented a higher level of social sophistication. For example, Alexander Joffe in his article "Alcohol and Social Complexity in Ancient Western Asia" posits that "the production, exchange, and consumption of alcoholic beverages form a significant element and regularity in the emergence of complex, hierarchically organized societies, along with the restructuring of labor and gender relations." For the major civilizations, then, one of the most important world events, the development of agriculture and the settling of societies, depended in part on the production, trade, consumption, and regulation of alcohol.

The very beginnings of human settlement show evidence of the domestication of grain and grape. Wild cereals and wild grapes grew in many areas. The existence of wild cereals facilitated the domestication of grains such as wheat and barley, which were used in the production of beer. Some historians argue that the production of beer even came before the production of bread. The argument asserts that the kind of wheat needed for bread did not exist during the beginnings of wheat cultivation. Evidence shows that the first kind of beer, however, was more like a nutritious gruel and had a very low alcohol content.

Humans produced wine during the Neolithic period, even before the domestication of grapes. Theoretically wine was easier to make than beer because merely crushing the grapes started the fermentation process for the wine. Humans improved grape vines through domestication in order to increase production and regulate the taste of the wine. Grape domestication normally occurred in an area where wild grapes already grew.

The cultivators then chose the vines that produced the best grapes and focused on those vines, cloning the best plants to optimize the harvests in the future. Beer, on the other hand, required sprouting or chewing the grain and then spitting it into a container in order to obtain fermentation. Anthropologists have argued that discovering wine gave hunter-gatherers a strong incentive to settle down to tend their vines. In other words, wine making actually led to settlement.

Grapes were not the only fruit humans used to produce wine. One of the most important plants for producing wine was the date palm. Humans began cultivating the date palm around the same time as they did the grapevine. These two, plus olives and figs, constituted the first four cultivated fruits. Some archeologists argue that figs, domesticated around 9500 BCE, could have been used for fermented beverages, since we have evidence that they were used later on for such. All four of these first fruits were definitively under cultivation by the Chalcolithic period, which dated from 3700 to 3200 BCE.

Scholars still debate where the very first wine was made. Wild grapes grew from the east coast of Spain to France, Tadzhikistan, and in valleys in southwest Central Asia. Some of the first kinds of wine came from these wild grapes. Toward the end of the fifth-millennium BCE grape culture spread to the Aegean, Mesopotamia, Syria, and Egypt. Other early evidence for domestic grape cultivation comes from the Chalcolithic period (3700–3200 BCE) and the Early Bronze Age (3200–1900 BCE) in the Levant, Northwestern Iraq, Israel, Lebanon, and Syria, although newer information shows that the first wine came much earlier, around 7000 BCE in China.

Some scholars argue that the very first evidence of wine making in the Middle East comes from an area in Western Iran, called Hajji Firuz Tepe, located in the Zagros mountains. Evidence has been found there that dates to between 5400 and 5000 BCE. Remains from wine have also been discovered in another part of Iran, Godin Tepe, dating from 3500 to 3000 BCE. Other scholars argue that the grape may have been brought to Godin Tepe from the Transcaucasia, the area between Asia and Europe, now the area of Southeastern Turkey, Armenia, and Azerbaijan. Still others argue that the earliest sign of wine making in the Aegean is from the end of the fifth millennium BCE, from eastern Macedonia in northern Greece. These grape pips, dating from 4460–4000 BCE, come from wild grapes or from plants at an early stage of domestication. Researchers also found waste products from wine production at Dikili Tash in Greece indicating that wild grapes were used for wine at the end of the fifth millennium-BCE. Moreover, pottery vessels have been discovered dating back to as early as around 6000 BCE. Therefore, people would have had the means to store juice that then fermented into wine. It is likely that grape growing for wine originated in many areas where a type of wine grape could easily be grown. In addition to evidence of wine production, evidence of alcohol consumption and accompanying feasting is found from the Early Bronze Age. For example, archeologists have found drinking vessels from around 3000 BCE.

Godin Tepe also shows remains of beer-drinking vessels. The beer was likely barley beer, and evidence shows that this was the earliest barley beer made in the world. Moreover, trading and likely political interchange took place between southern Mesopotamia and Godin Tepe because Godin was located on the very important East/West trade route between the Mediterranean and China, the Silk Road. This region is also known for the first writing system, the first code of law, and the first bureaucracy, linking the development of wine and beer production, trade, consumption, and regulation to these important social and political developments in the ancient world.

Moreover, alcohol influenced the development of the ancient civilizations of Egypt, Mesopotamia, China, India, and the Americas. The production and sale of alcohol shaped gender as well as elite and lower-class identities. The consumption of alcohol structured everything from daily nutrition and medicine to social hierarchies and religious rituals, and the regulation of alcohol helped both to regulate trade as it spread and to support governments with taxes.

Two of the first civilizations in the Middle East, Egypt and Mesopotamia, also known as the river valley civilizations, developed along the Nile River and in the area between the Tigris and Euphrates rivers respectively. Egyptian culture was a more uniform culture. Mesopotamia, in contrast, was a disparate civilization, made up of many cultures, including the Sumerians, Akkadians, and Hittites. The characteristics of these two Pre-Classical societies included permanency, regional trade, social hierarchy, governmental regulation, and a religious belief system. The production, trade, consumption, and regulation of alcohol were infused in all of these societal characteristics. The production and trade of alcoholic beverages in Egypt and Mesopotamia facilitated the growth of the economies in those areas. The consumption patterns of alcohol in Mesopotamia and Egypt affected social formation, while the regulation of alcohol shaped political development in those areas.

Egypt

The production, trade, consumption, and regulation of alcohol significantly shaped the growing Egyptian civilization. Production of wine by elites and beer by commoners helped to define class differences. Trade of alcohol by women, both wine in taverns and beer in the market, helped to shape gender ideologies. Consumption of alcohol structured social gatherings, religious rituals, daily sustenance, and the composition of medicine. Social treatises on alcohol singled out particular groups, perpetuating the social hierarchy. Finally, regulations solidified the role of government in the creation of commercial standards, and taxes provided for the growth of government.

The River Valley civilization of Egypt was established after roughly 4000 BCE. Central to the stability of the civilization was its sustenance, especially the excess food production that allowed the civilization to flourish. Part of the food production included wine and beer. Alcohol became so important, in fact, that Egyptians created a god of wine, Dionysus. Egyptians first began purchasing wine from elsewhere before they began producing it themselves. Wild grapes did not grow naturally in Egypt; the dry climate made wine production more difficult. By 3000 BCE, however, vines were distributed throughout the Middle East and the eastern Mediterranean, making wine accessible to Egypt. Early evidence of wine comes from the tomb of an Egyptian king who lived around 3150 BCE; his tomb contained hundreds of wine jars with remnants of resin inside each of them. In virtually all cases, elites, such as kings and priests, cultivated wine in walled gardens, and there existed a royal winemaking industry in the Nile Delta. Domestic grape vines were fairly rare, labor intensive, and took several years to produce, therefore they needed a significant capital investment. In Egypt vineyards likely needed to be irrigated as well. These difficulties in production meant wine was a luxury item. Wine's production and trade as a luxury item helped to diversify the economy in ancient Egypt and established wine use as a notable characteristic of elite culture.

Most Egyptian wines came from the area of the Delta, although little was exported because not enough was produced to export. Egyptians likely produced both white and red wines. Illustrations on tombs from the Old Kingdom show the beginnings of the wine-production industry. Egyptians made grape wine by putting grapes into vats and then treading on them in order to extract the juice. The vats were round in shape and large enough to hold four to six men to stomp the grapes. The vintner sometimes hired musicians to play while the men stomped. The stompers either held onto poles erected above the vats, or held onto the hips of each other to keep their balance. The grapes were about ankle deep in the vats, and the juice flowed out through a bung on the side of the vat into smaller vats. After the workers stomped most of the juice out of the grapes, they put the lees, or the dregs, into a cloth bag, then tied both ends of the cloth to poles and twisted the poles to wring out the last of the juice.

After pressing the juice, the workers strained it through cloth and put it into fermentation jars about two and a half feet tall, the insides of which had been smeared with resin. The resin aided in the preservation of the wine. The mouth of the fermentation jar had a rounded lip and was about 6 inches in diameter; while the body was about 10 inches at its widest. Sometimes the workers heated the jars to speed up the fermentation process. After fermentation, a vintner put the wine into decanters, small ones for religious use and larger ones for daily, household use. He then sealed the containers with straw and clay and stamped them with the official stamps, which had the year of the king's rule, the district, the name of the wine, and sometimes the name of the vintner. Sometimes he poured the wine into skins, especially if the wine was to be carried long distances. Finally, by the time of the New Kingdom (1550–1069 BCE) the vintner impressed his imprimatur, or license, into the stopper. The first imprimatur became more and more detailed as the craft became more professionalized.

After sealing the wine the wine maker then drilled safety holes into the toppers or into the necks to prevent the containers from bursting. He then plugged them with straw, wax, or clay. After awhile he tasted the wine to assess its quality, and then marked the grade on the lids. Wine was labeled good, twice good, three times good, and sweet, twice sweet, and so on. Labeling also told the age of the wine. Other kinds of labeling included wine for taxes and wine for offerings, both indicating that wine had become profitable for the government and important in religious rituals. Finally, the vessels, tapered at the end, were stored leaning and stacked against a wall.

Egyptian wine did not last long; people drank it within a year. It was also very sweet because the sugar content of the grapes was very high. High sugar content occurred because of the dry climate, which meant the grapes were probably shriveled and therefore they could not ferment all the sugar into alcohol and they remained sweet. In addition to regular sweet wine, Egyptians made mixed or spiced wines, flavoring them with juices, herbs, and spices. Egyptians also made palm wine. Palm wine came from oases and palm-growing areas. People tapped into the top of a date palm tree to gather its sap. The sap fermented very quickly because of the hot weather.

Wine was not only made for personal use, but it was also sold in taverns. Most tavern owners as well as tavern employees were women, and many of the women who worked in taverns were prostitutes. As a result, taverns had reputations as houses of prostitution and any woman associated with a tavern was suspect. So as early as ancient Egypt, society began to stereotype as immoral most women who associated with alcohol, especially in public. This same correlation was not applied to men, of course, and elite women, by virtue of their class, escaped the characterization in Egypt.

In addition to wine, beer, too, had an impact on Egyptian society. The beginnings of beer go back to around the fourth-millennium BCE. By 3000 BCE beer was more widespread and in larger production than wine. Beer could be made at any time, unlike wine, which could only be made during the grape harvest. And beer, like bread, could be made in people's homes. Moreover, the grain could be stored and was more portable than grapes. Unlike modern beer, the beer of ancient Egypt was more like food. It was made from either red, white, or black barley, or emmer wheat, and was opaque, thick, and more like soup or gruel. Making barley beer began with moistening barley and laying it out for one day, then moistening it and drying it again while it was in a vessel. After it dried, the beer maker shook it in the sun until it fell apart. Then he or she ground it and made it into loaves adding leaven to make it rise. Workers cooked it for just a little while and then dissolved sweetened water into it and pushed it through a sieve.

Another way to make beer consisted of pouring moistened grain into a mortar, grinding it, adding yeast, then cooking the dough over a slow fire until it was partially baked. Next, the beer maker broke the partially baked bread into pieces and left them to soak in water for several days. He or she then placed the pieces into large human-sized fermentation vats and stomped them into gruel, poured the gruel into a wide-woven basket that was placed over a large jar, and then kneaded it so the liquid could flow through the basket into the jar. Next the maker poured the liquid into large beer jars, sometimes adding dates or date juice to flavor the beer and sugar for fermentation. The beer usually did not have a high alcohol content, perhaps between 4 and 5 percent, although because it was brewed in each home the alcohol content could vary. In the later dynasties, when money came into use, women sold beer in the markets to both men and women. Since women made beer at home for their families, they likely made an excess of beer to sell in the markets. Egyptian society normalized women's roles as beer makers, easily accepting their transition into beer peddlers. The almost exclusive involvement of women in beer production and trade characterized those activities as feminine, creating a defining feature of female gender identity, which in this case was not sexually related.

In addition to influencing gender identity, alcohol in ancient Egypt structured social occasions and religious ceremonies, and prominently figured in daily sustenance and medicine. Elite Egyptians entertained with wine. Many depictions exist of elite banquets where excessive wine drinking took place by both elite men and women. H. F. Lutz's *Viticulture and Brewing in the Ancient Orient* describes a typical party. To begin, a wooden image of a dead person was paraded around the gathering to show that death could come at any time so one should enjoy oneself while it was still possible. Taking their cue from the performance, guests felt free to overindulge in wine. Tomb paintings show that both elite men and women drank to excess; they display pictures of passed out men being carried away by their servants and women vomiting while their heads were held by their female servants. One elite woman was reported to have said "Give me eighteen cups of wine ... don't you see I want to get drunk! My insides are as dry as straw." Society saw wine consumption, even excessive consumption, as a characteristic of the rich, helping to define elite identity, an identity that categorized women by their privilege before their gender.

Wine also shaped Egyptian religion. Many myths surrounded wine in Egypt. Egyptians believed that the reproduction of the vine was the work of the god Osiris, representing his rebirth. Ancient Egyptians commonly offered up wine to the gods. Festivals for the god Dionysus as well as for other gods featured wine. During the New Kingdom when Egypt was very wealthy as a result of Thutmose III, alcohol use during religious festivals soared. The king granted more money to the priests to provide wine for daily temple rituals; and bread and beer were also required twice a day as offerings to the dead god-king at funeral temples. Priests poured wine libations onto the ground as well as drank much of the wine themselves. Staff members of the temples as well as priests and others consumed large quantities of beer in the daily temple rituals as well as in the temple festivals. The annual cat-goddess festival, which drew worshipers from all over Egypt, included excessive alcoholic celebrations by men, women, and children. One of the subsequent kings, Akhenaton, had a yearly festival dedicated to the god Amon for which the king took a state journey to his temple at Karnak. The yearly ritual could last up to a month, and both beer and wine were drunk to excess during the entire festival.

Beer, too, held symbolic meaning in Egypt. For example, the feline goddess Hathor-Sekhmet was supposedly appeased with red-dyed beer in order to save humans from her rage. She was credited with the origin of beer, and her temple was known as the "house of drunkenness." Moreover, Egyptians believed that when men dreamed about beer, each dream held a special meaning. If a man dreamed of sweet beer it was good luck. If he dreamed of bakery beer he would live a long life, or if he dreamed of stored beer he would be healed if sick. If a man dreamed of drinking warm beer he would soon be suffering, or if he dreamed of brewing beer in his own home he would soon be banished from his house. In addition, if a man was having bad dreams he could be cured by rubbing his body with herbs moistened with beer and having a spell uttered over him.

Beer was also an essential part of daily sustenance. Bread and beer were staples for Egyptians from all classes. Beer was even called ancient Egypt's "national drink." It was nutritious; it contained many calories as well as protein, B vitamins, and live yeast. Because it constituted a daily necessity, the government used beer as wages. It paid soldiers through rations of loaves of bread and jugs of beer. Non-military laborers were paid in the same way. A basic wage for an ordinary laborer consisted of ten loaves of bread and anywhere from one-third to two jugs of beer, with an average of about two and a half liters. Higher ranking workers also received bread and beer rations, but in double or triple the quantity. In addition to the army and laborers, priests in temples received an allotted amount of beer for food. Since most beer was drunk for daily sustenance, excess drinking was rare. Beer was considered more of a necessary food than a recreational alcohol. Men ate bread, beer, and onions for lunch. Children and nursing mothers drank beer for health and nutritional reasons.

Hosts commonly provided bread and beer for their guests, and were considered rude if they did not. Offering beer, then, became a symbol of polite society, conferring social capital on those who could afford the gesture. Clearly the wealthy had more ability than poorer people to provide drink to their guests, and thus lack of access to abundant alcohol caused poorer people to have fewer opportunities to become respected members of polite society.

Egyptians also believed in the curative properties of beer and wine. One of the most famous sources for Egyptian medicine, the Papyrus Ebers, which was written about 1500 BCE, is a collection of remedies from as early as 3400 BCE. All of these remedies contained some form of alcohol. One prescription to stop constipation consisted of chewing the berry from a castor oil tree together with drinking some beer. Another prescription for a diuretic called for water from the bird pond, a swill of beer, and fresh milk. Healers could make a purgative from an onion beaten up in the froth of beer, and cure an inflamed abdomen with a mixture of bread of the zizyphus lotus flower, cat's dung, red lead, watermelon, sweet beer, and wine made into a plaster and put onto the abdomen. For problems of the anus, a mixture of cowhorn, pieces of dried oil, and yeast of wine were made into a suppository. To dress a wound, crushed human excrement mixed with the yeast of sweet beer, sefet-oil, and honey were applied to the area. Beer was used to wash down herbs, to rub on the body, and as a mouthwash, an enema, and a douche. Many more remedies existed that included some form of either beer or wine.

Alcohol use in Egyptian society led in some cases to abuse, resulting in socially prescriptive treatises penned by prominent writers and thinkers that pointed to the damage caused by going to beer houses. They also argued against over-indulging in beer and wine, even during times of mourning. For example, Ani, an Egyptian sage, said "Do not pass [thy time] in the beer-house and don't indulge in drinking beer, lest you utter evil speech and don't know what you're saying. Then if thou fallest to the ground and thou breakest the limbs, none reacheth out the hand to help thee. Behold, thy companions! They drink and say: Go home, thou, who has drunk enough!" (as quoted in Lutz, *Viticulture and Brewing in the Ancient Orient*). Moreover, proscriptive works written by Ani and Amenehotep discouraged students from excessive drinking either at home or at inns. It was believed that students would "forsakest books [and] ... abandon thyself to pleasure." These sages also warned against alcoholism and alcohol-related personality problems. At the same time, however, judgments around alcohol were class specific. Elites looked down upon others who over-indulged, and in particular disparaged tavern keepers. Yet there were many stories of elite banquets after which people had to be carried home by their servants.

In addition to treatises on moderation, the government regulated the quality of wine and levied a wine tax. Inspectors tasted the wines in taverns and markets to regulate the prices and quality of wine. The state also earned substantial revenues from customs duties on foreign wine coming into Egypt. One-sixth of the yield of Egyptian vineyards went to pay taxes except those that were owned by the temples or by the king. These numerous wine taxes were vital to the state treasury as well as to the temples. So the taxes and regulations as well as the production, trade, and numerous uses of alcohol reveal how it permeated all areas of Egyptian society.

Mesopotamia

The production, trade, consumption, and regulation of alcohol in Mesopotamia helped shape many areas in that civilization. Beer production differentiated male and female work roles. In addition, the growing beer trade led to the pro-fessionalization of traders, and the vibrant regional trade in alcohol, especially wine, expanded trade networks. Moreover, alcohol consumption patterns created class identity, and even differentiated elites from each other. Alcohol was so central to Mesopotamian society that the famous Hammurabic Code of 2225 BCE included many laws regulating the trade.

Ancient southern Mesopotamia was a center of beer-drinking culture. Archeologists have even uncovered an ancient brewery that included tanks for making beer bread. Moreover, jars and drinking tubes for beer were found in tombs, and pictures of beer drinking at banquets and during sexual intercourse were found on cylinder seals. Significantly, one of the first uses of writing in Sumerian culture was the record of a beer recipe, which was written in cuneform around 3500 BCE.

Mesopotamians produced beer from malted barley; they did not have hops. Barley beer was the most common beverage in ancient Sumer because the hot and dry climate was conducive to grain growing. Beer making was very labor intensive, required gender-specific tasks, and coincided with bread making. The beer maker, usually a man, began by crushing grain with a wooden pestle in order to loosen the husks. Then the miller, usually a woman, crushed the grain with a smaller stone. Next, a man mixed the dough by standing in a large vat and kneading it with his feet. Then the dough was made into little cakes, and sometimes dates were added for flavor. The cakes were then allowed to rise. Afterward, another man pressed the dough cakes through a sieve into a large vat, added water, and then poured it into clay jars and sealed them. Over time, brewers changed the ingredients of beer; they began to add spices to improve the taste. The beer was strained to remove sediment and floating grains from it and then many brewers put the beer into leather bags or in clay barrels or jars.

Beer production helped in the development of specialized occupations. Beer making was so individualized that each brewer carried his own unique clay vats with him when he traveled. The cracks in the vats contained yeast, which gave each particular beer its special flavor. Carrying vats also identified brewers by their profession as they traveled. Moreover, beer was so significant in Mesopotamian culture that the brewers' craft was the only one to enjoy divine protection from a goddess – in fact from two female figures – Nin and Siris. Siris was known as the divine patron of the brewer in Mesopotamia.

The Babylonians made both beer and wine, though, and engaged in the alcohol trade. In Babylonia the customer supplied the grain and the brewer supplied the manufacturing equipment, which included the vats, fermenting tubs, barrels, jars, and the brewer's furnace. Babylonians also made wine from date palms. In one method the winemaker scratched the stem of the date plant with a sharp knife and gathered the sap into jars and let it ferment. In another method the winemaker pressed the fresh dates and then left the juice to ferment. Date wine from the stem spoiled within a few hours, but the wine made from the actual dates lasted much longer. Babylonians also made pomegranate wine and liquor from figs. Babylonians made grape wine as well, but produced it only in the dry-farming agricultural areas to the north and west of Babylonia. Unlike beer, though, grape wine could be made only once a year, when the grapes ripened. Wine had a longer shelf life than beer if the wine was kept in sealed jars, which typically held several gallons each.

Since so little wine was produced in Babylonia, most wine came from trade with Syria. The trade in wine helped to develop and expand crucial trading networks in the region as well. In the first-millennium BCE the Damascus region became famous for its wine. This trade increased with the domestication of the camel, and became very important in Mesopotamia along the Euphrates.

Alcohol consumption patterns influenced even more areas in society. Wine was an expensive and rare commodity, which meant that it became an elite drink and its consumption yet another characteristic of the privileged. As a luxury item, wine was served only to the gods and the wealthy. Tablets from the eighth-century BCE reveal the scarcity of wine when noting the wine ration for the royal household to be less than a half pint per person. In areas where vines were easily cultivated, such as Greece, however, wine drinking was more widespread and represented to a lesser degree a class-specific beverage. Yet it was still associated with elites more so than with the lower classes, because even in Greece it cost a regular laborer almost two days' wages to buy one liter.

In Babylonia since grape wine was so expensive poorer people drank cheap date wine. Even into the later Pre-Classical period, during the Hittite Kingdom, 1700–1050 BCE, wine was still used mostly for rituals and festivals, such as for soldiers who were giving their oath of loyalty, for the founding of a new palace, or for supplicating the gods. In the Hittite Kingdom elites drank grape wine and pomegranate wine, both of which were very expensive. Some scholars argue that elites diluted their wine with water, usually half and half, and considered those who did not dilute their wine to be unsophisticated. People diluted their wine likely because the hot climate did not allow for their thirst to be quenched with straight wine, and since potable water was not common, Babylonians believed that mixing water with wine sanitized it and prevented illness. Moreover, elites used wine during the Bronze Age to differentiate status within elite society. Elites utilized wine in "competitive consumption." For example, elites in the Middle Bronze Age competed with each other by throwing lavish, wine-saturated feasts in order to demonstrate their wealth, solidify alliances, and gain the support or loyalty of others.

In contrast to the elite nature of wine, the masses drank beer in ancient southern Mesopotamia. Beer constituted a significant part of the daily diet and was included on the ration lists for palace workers, who received the equivalent of one quart to one gallon of beer per day, depending on their rank. People also drank beer as they socialized in taverns. They drank from a common vat usually through drinking tubes with small perforated holes on the end that acted as strainers to remove solids such as the hulls of the malted barley. Communal beer drinking facilitated camaraderie among patrons, and as drinking it was associated mainly with commoners, it also became a characteristic of lower-class identity.

Alcohol regulation differed by kingdom in Mesopotamia. In the period between 4100 BCE and 3100 BCE, the state controlled the coerced labor that made the beer. In Sumeria the government regulated the quality and measurements of beer. Beer makers had to make no less than the legal amount of beer based on the weight of ingredients given to them by the customer, thus keeping beer makers from cheating the customer. Another regulation stipulated that a barmaid who served watered-down beer would be dunked in water. The Hammurabic Code, created under the Babylonian king, Hammurabi, in

2225 BCE, regulated the proper behavior for tavern owners and those who frequented taverns. For example, the price of beer was set for tavern keepers, who were overwhelmingly women. Regulations allowed credit in the taverns and repayment was a set amount of corn from the customer's harvest. A tavernness had to accept payment for drinks in corn. If she demanded money instead, and the money that she demanded for the drink was greater than the value of the corn, then she would be thrown in the water. Hammurabi also wrote that if a priestess tried to open a tavern, or if she even entered a tavern with the idea of drinking, she was to be immediately burned to death. Moreover, if would-be traitors met in a tavern, and the tavern keeper did not report them, she would be held responsible for their actions and executed. These law codes regulating taverns indicate the role of the government in regulating business, the ubiquity of taverns in Babylonia, as well as the role of taverns as social centers where men gathered and talked politics. Finally, the codes referred to tavern keepers as women, showing that the occupation had become feminized, resulting in gender ideologies that constructed socially acceptable occupations for men and women in Babylonia.

In addition to the Hammurabic code, a later kingdom, the Hittites, created laws specifically to protect the labor intensive and irrigated vineyards. For example, the penalty for the theft of a vine or tendril involved some form of corporal punishment along with the fine of a shekel of silver. There were also fines and punishments for burning down a vineyard, letting one's sheep into a productive vineyard, stealing tendrils from a fenced-in vineyard, or for cutting down a vine. The Hittites also had several laws regulating the price of wine. These regulations reflected the high value of vineyards, and indeed wine, in the Hittite Kingdom.

Jewish society

One of the world's major religions, Judaism, grew out of an area within Mesopotamia. The Jewish people were nomadic, first migrating to an area encompassed by present-day Israel/Palestine and Lebanon, called Canaan, then to Egypt, and then back to Canaan. Judaism followed the Hebrew Bible, in which wine figured prominently. According to the Old Testament (divided and numbered differently than the Hebrew Bible) wine possessed symbolic power, strengthened social relations, and brought happiness. Abuse of wine, however, brought illness, public wrongdoing, and lack of ability to honor God. The Bible praised the moderate use of alcohol, although overindulgence was a sin. To begin with, the Bible mentioned alcohol more than 220 times. Genesis said that God blessed his people with grain and wine, and connected drinking wine with eating food. The Bible also saw wine as a gift from God. Moreover, Psalms stated: "Thou dost cause the grass to grow for the cattle, And Plants for man to cultivate, That he may bring forth food from the earth, And wine to gladden the heart of man, ... " (As quoted in Hewitt, *A Biblical Perspective on the Use and Abuse of Alcohol and Other*

Drugs.) In many places the Bible also equated good hospitality with providing wine for one's guests. Kings served wine to their guests as accorded into the book of Esther: "Wine was served in golden cups of various patterns: the king's wine flowed freely as befitted a king ... " In other places the Bible stated that wine brought happiness. For example, the Book of Judges stated: "new wine ... gladdens gods and men." Song of Solomon stated: "Eat, friends, and drink, until you are drunk with love." Moreover, Jews used wine in all major rituals; circumcisions, weddings, Passover Seder, and Purim – where sanctioned overconsumption took place. Jews gave wine as gifts, used it in celebrations of victory, provided it as a reward for work, and recommended it as a way to honor a king. It was used as an offering to God, a tithe to the church, a gift to priests from parishioners, and a reward from God to his followers.

In many places the Bible warned against using too much alcohol. The story of Lot explained that he drank too much wine, leading him to have intercourse with his daughters. Deuteronomy stated that drunkards were to be severely punished, and Proverbs stated that if one gulped down wine "then your eyes see strange sights, your wits and your speech are confused; you become like a man tossing out at sea ... " Many other passages condemned drunkenness, listing its many ills. It could make one sick, weak, ill, violent, irresponsible, lustful, anxious, and apathetic. It could also lead to a lack of self-control, fights, gossip, poverty, and exile. Most importantly the book of Isaiah admonished that it could lead one to neglect God's work: "[those] inflamed with wine ... have no eyes for the work of the Lord." So the Jewish religion recommended moderation and cautioned against abuse, but more importantly it relied on wine, giving it symbolic power to shape important rituals and celebrations that defined that culture.

China

Alcohol began influencing Chinese civilization earlier than anywhere else in the world. It structured important religious and social ceremonies, established itself as a common medium for healing, and led to significant political turmoil. Legends from the Xia Dynasty, 2140–1711 BCE, explained the beginnings of alcohol in China. One story told of a young woman named Yi Di who tasted fermented grain and subsequently felt elated. She then gave it to Emperor Yu who drank it. He proclaimed that Yi Di must be exiled because of the probable ill effects of alcohol on his kingdom. Another legend told of Du Kang, a young shepherd, again from the Xia Dynasty, who when caught in a rainstorm one day up on a mountain, quickly herded his sheep home and as a result forgot his lunch of cooked and husked sorghum that he had left hanging in a tree. When he returned after a few days the fermented lunch tasted very good and gave him a good feeling. He and his family continued to make alcohol and he has been called the "God of alcohol." These two legends reveal how differently Chinese society viewed women and alcohol versus men and alcohol. The female in the first legend was condemned, while the male in the second legend was rewarded, showing how the cultural meanings of alcohol worked together with gender ideologies to shape gender hierarchies in China.

The actual beginnings of alcohol occurred much earlier than the Xia dynasty. The earliest wine, or fermented liquor, came from China, predating Middle Eastern alcohol by a few thousand years. Archeologists have found pottery shards showing remnants of rice and grape wine dating back to 7000 BCE in Jiahu village in Henan Province. Evidence from a later period shows that fermented alcoholic beverages were also made from millet and rice. Moreover, major excavations along the Yellow River found various kinds of serving goblets that implied the use of fermented beverages during the periods of Erlitou (ca. 1900–1500 BCE), Shang (ca. 1600–1046 BCE), and Western Zhou (ca. 1046–771 BCE).

The Chinese produced most alcohol by using one part black millet and two parts rice mixed together. The mixture was cooked over an open fire in a clay vessel. Workers poured boiling water over rice and added human saliva to begin fermentation. They then let it ferment for five to seven days. In another method workers first milled rice to remove any rough surfaces (in order to make a clearer product), then steamed the rice and spread it out to dry. Next, they made a mash and added ingredients for fermentation. They finally added spices such as pepper to flavor the alcohol. In general alcohol was brewed in the winter and drank in the spring, which leads to the conclusion that it kept for a relatively long period of time.

By the Shang dynasty, which was between 1600 and 1046 BCE, three kinds of alcohol existed: chang, which was an herbal wine; li, which was a sweet, low-alcoholic millet or rice wine; and jiu, which had a high alcohol content of 10 to 15 percent. The later Zhou period, 1046–256 BCE, saw two more kinds of alcoholic beverages called luo, which was fermented from fruit; and lao, which was unfiltered rice or millet wine. The many varieties of wine point to its prevalence in that civilization.

Alcohol shaped religious and cultural ceremonies in ancient China. The Chinese believed that consuming wine allowed them to communicate with the spirit world. Mourners drank to intoxication during burial ceremonies to communicate both with the deceased and with the gods, and alcohol accompanied elites into the next life. Moreover, elites performed elaborate sacrifices that included excessive feasting and drinking, and the king used wine in sacrifices to honor the ancestors.

One of the most important ancient Chinese ceremonies was the ancestor ceremony where wine and food were offered to the ancestors. Patrick McGovern describes this ceremony in *Uncorking the Past: the Quest for Wine, Beer, and Other Alcoholic Beverages*. After four days of fasting a descendent of the deceased, called the shi, was chosen to communicate with the ancestors. Usually the shi was a grandson or a daughter-in-law. After seven days of fasting by the shi there was a feast in the temple for the deceased where the shi drank nine cups of warmed wine. Then the shi offered food and wine to the deceased and afterward ate and drank for the deceased.

Alcohol constructed other rituals as well, and even led to political intrigue. Rites of passage such as manhood and marriage were organized around alcohol. The manhood ceremony featured offerings of alcoholic beverages and food to the ancestors, the mother, and the other relatives and guests at the ceremony. In the wedding ceremony the bride's family offered wine to the groom's parents, symbolizing their acceptance of the marriage. Alcohol became so prevalent in Chinese society that some argue that the downfall of the Shang dynasty was caused by the emperor's perpetual drunkenness. He was reputedly a tyrant who had frequent drunken orgies. Thus he lost the "Mandate of Heaven," or the right to rule, and was deposed.

Alcohol's influence in Chinese culture spread even further. It contributed to the development of Chinese medicine. The ancient Chinese believed in the power of alcohol to heal. For example, Bernard Read in *Chinese Materia Medica* noted that in order to cure apoplexy, fistula, stomach or heart pain, colic, hemorrhoids, worm toxemia, flatulence, and bleeding from the bowel a mixture of pit viper placed in a gallon of wine, which had been buried for a year under a horse's stall, was to be used. Moreover, using donkey's placenta in wine cured alcoholism, and lizard's liver, the skin of a cicada locust, and wine made into a poultice induced abortions, while chicken brains in alcohol and a chicken's claw in wine eased a difficult labor and stopped convulsions by infants. Furthermore, eating chicken intestines with alcohol cured incontinence and frequent urination, and according to Salvatore P. Lucia in *A History of Wine as Therapy*, drinking a combination of 12 herbs, including cinnamon, and ground oyster shells dissolved in warm wine stopped a heart attack. The power of wine to heal, along with its strong symbolism, made it a potent medium in Chinese society.

India

Pre-Classical India, or the early Vedic period, dates back as early as 2500 BCE. During that period Indians produced a fermented alcoholic beverage called soma, which shaped both religious beliefs and cultural practices. Indians equated soma with the gods, and thought of it as a deity in liquid form. Women commonly produced soma in their homes, but the sacred production of soma was highly ritualistic. The roots of a leafless milkweed vine had to be pulled by the light of the moon and then hauled in a goat-pulled cart to a sacrificial place. Priests crushed the vines into a sieve made of wool and then pressed them into a liquid, which was then mixed with either sweet or sour milk or curds and flour. It took nine days to ferment. The Rig-Veda includes many odes to soma (as quoted in Lucia, *A History of Wine as Therapy*):

> O Soma, You have been crushed, you flow as a stream to Indra, scattering joy on all sides, you bestow immortal food. Seven women stir thee with

their fingers blending their voices in a song to thee, you remind the sacrificer of his duties at the sacrifice. Of all the drinks that Indra has, you are the most pleasant and intoxicating. This is Soma, who flows wine, who is strength giving.

This ode glorifies both soma and women's role in its production. Women's connection to alcohol appeared to add to their status in Indian society.

The symbolic power of soma in ancient Indian society led to the belief in its curative powers. The Rig-Veda, one of the sacred texts of Hinduism from the early Vedic period, included medical remedies using soma. Moreover, soma structured many of the rituals in the Hindu religion. For example, soma was used as an offering to the gods, and it was written that drinking soma brought on immortality. Furthermore, it was commonly believed that the gods, especially Indra and Agni, drank soma. In Hinduism ambivalence existed toward soma, however. In some writings it seemed to be accepted, and in others it was not, depending upon the time period. The Bhagaved-gita argued that only those with "demoniac mentality" drank. Ayurveda, a medical practice based on Hindu principles, used alcohol in some of its remedies. So whether or not alcohol consumption was accepted or not remained unresolved in Hinduism. While many contradictions existed regarding alcohol, alcohol consumption and regulation helped to shape society and religion in ancient India.

The Americas

The first known site of humans in the Americas is located at Monte Verde in Chile. It dates back to about 11,000 BCE. While no definitive evidence of alcoholic beverages had been found by the early twenty-first-century, people inhabited the area year round and had access to edible berries and bulrush, both of which could be fermented. Later on, with the domestication of corn, alcohol production became widespread. Corn beer, or chicha, which was made by women, became the most important fermented beverage in the Andean region. There is evidence of pottery dating back to 3000 BCE that was likely used for chicha. Chicha constituted the bulk of daily sustenance for many Andeans. Moreover, they considered it to be sacred, believing it came from the earth goddess. Since only women brewed chicha it became a fundamental part of their identity as women, giving them a role that included not only producing a life-sustaining substance, but also reproducing the very culture of the people.

Conclusion

Production, trade, consumption, and regulation of alcohol helped construct the economic, social, cultural, and political development of early civilizations. First, all these civilizations showed evidence of alcohol production. The virtually universal desire for alcohol from the very beginnings of civilization led to ancient societies creating alcohol out of whatever was available. For example, in Egypt and Mesopotamia grain was plentiful and therefore it was made into beer, which became the most common alcoholic drink in those civilizations. The date palm was also plentiful in those areas and was therefore made into date palm wine. In China rice and millet were readily available and so they were made into wine; in India milkweed was available and so it was made into soma, and in the Americas corn was available and so it was made into chicha. Second, the alcohol trade opened up routes and diversified economic development in Egypt and Mesopotamia, and led to the professionalization of brewers in Mesopotamia.

Third, many cultures, including Egypt, Mesopotamia, India, and the Americas considered alcohol to be a sacred substance and thus ritualized its production in order to reinforce its revered position in society. Fourth, alcohol helped create gender identities. Egyptian society labeled women who sold alcohol in taverns as prostitutes (some, but not all, were), so women's connection to alcohol in that case resulted in a negative gender stereotype. In Egypt, Mesopotamia, and the Americas women brewed beer, thus identifying beer production as feminine and giving women the power to sustain both life and culture. In Mesopotamia male brewers identified themselves as professional artisans as they traveled around, making the professionalization of brewing essentially masculine. In China legends credited a woman in one case, and a man in another, with the discovery of alcohol. The fate of the woman, however, was exile, while that of the man fame and fortune, suggesting that alcohol enhanced male identity but diminished female identity. In all of these cases the origins, production, and trade of alcohol were gendered, helping to define gender ideologies across many civilizations.

Consumption of alcohol helped to define social status, and structure nourishment, medicine, and religious and social rituals throughout the ancient world. First, consumption practices characterized one's place in the social hierarchy. In Egypt and most of Mesopotamia elites had much more access to wine than did the lower classes, thus drinking wine became a characteristic of elite identity. Moreover, the lavish, alcohol-filled parties thrown by elites reinforced their social status. In contrast, in Egypt and Mesopotamia the lower classes drank beer because it was very plentiful; it therefore became part of lower-class culture and identity. Second, in Egypt, Mesopotamia, and the Americas beer was essential to daily sustenance. It was such a staple in the diets of Egyptians and Mesopotamians that it was used as payment for workers and given in rations to soldiers. Third, alcohol helped define medicine. Many civilizations including Egypt, China, and India believed alcohol to be a powerful substance, and used it in almost every cure.

Fourth, alcohol structured social rituals in Egypt, Mesopotamia (including Jewish culture), and China. In Egypt the definition of politeness meant offering alcohol to guests, and in Mesopotamia taverns shaped social life. In Jewish culture alcohol shaped such social rituals as weddings and circumcisions, while in China alcohol structured the ancestor ceremony and marriage ceremonies. Fifth, in Egypt, Mesopotamia, China, India, and the Americas alcohol framed religious beliefs and rituals. Egyptians believed in a god of wine, and that the growth of grapes represented the rebirth of their god Osiris. Alcohol also made up most of their offerings to the gods. In Jewish society wine possessed symbolic power, while the Chinese believed in the power of alcohol as a conduit to the gods, and Indians believed that soma led to immortality. In the Americas Andeans believed that chicha was sacred, given to them by the earth goddess. In all these societies alcohol shaped important aspects of both society and culture.

Alcohol regulation helped standardize trade, define acceptable social mores, and provide governments with essential resources. First, Egypt and Mesopotamia regulated many aspects surrounding the sale of alcohol to ensure fair business practices, giving government an important role in developing a commercial culture. Second, in both Egypt and Mesopotamia (including Jewish culture), prescriptive literature outlined appropriate drinking behavior, especially for certain segments of society, reinforcing social structures and perpetuating social hierarchies. Third, governments came to rely on alcohol taxes as stable income, crucial for governmental stability.

Alcohol gave people the impetus to settle down and form the early agricultural civilizations. Alcohol also shaped the development of ancient societies. People treated it as sacred, believing it to be connected to the gods. It helped signify class and gender identities, as societies characterized the elite and the lower class, as well as women and men in part by their relationship to alcohol. Alcohol structured religious and social rituals as well as daily meals, and defined most medical practice. Finally, its taxes helped maintain and perpetuate ancient governments. Alcohol permeated virtually all areas of the ancient world.

Further reading

Ancient Egyptian Medicine: The Papyrus Ebers. Translated by Cyril P. Bryan. 1930. Chicago: Ares Publishers.

Darby, William, J. Paul Ghalioungui, and Louis Grivetti. 1976. *Food: The Gift of Osiris.* Vol. 2. London: Academic Press.

Davies, W. W. 1905. *The Codes of Hammurabi and Moses.* Cincinnati, OH: Jennings and Graham.

Dayagi-Mendels, M. 1999. *Drink and Be Merry: Wine and Beer in Ancient Times.* Jerusalem: The Israel Museum.

Geller, J. 1993. "Bread and Beer in Fourth-Millennium Egypt." *Food and Foodways.* 5 (3): 255–67.

Hartman, L. F. and A. L. Oppenheim. 1950. "On Beer and Brewing Techniques in Ancient Mesopotamia." *Journal of the American Oriental Society.* 10: 1–55.

Joffe, A. H. 1998. "Alcohol and Social Complexity in Ancient Western Asia." *Current Anthropology.* 39 (3): 297–322.

Lucia, S. P. M. D. 1963. *A History of Wine as Therapy.* Philadelphia: J. B. Lippincott Company.

Lutz, H. F. 1922. *Viticulture and Brewing in The Ancient Orient.* New York: G. E. Stechert & Co.

McGovern, P. E. 2003. *Ancient Wine: The Search for the Origins of Viniculture.* Princeton, NJ: Princeton University Press.

McGovern P. E. 2009. *Uncorking the Past: The Quest for Wine, Beer and Other Alcoholic Beverages.* Berkeley: University of California Press.

McGovern, P. E., E. D. Butrym, A. Nunez, C. S. Wang, M. P. Richards, R. A. Moreau, J. G. Tang, J. Z. Zhang, G. R. Hall, and Z. Q. Zhang 2004. "Fermented Beverages of Pre- and Proto-Historic China." In *Proceedings of the National Academy of Sciences.* November: www.pnas.org cgi/doi/10.1073/pnas.0407921102 (accessed December 13, 2011).

McGovern, P. E., S. J. Fleming and S. Katz (eds.) 1996. *The Origins and Ancient History of Wine.* Amsterdam: Gordon and Breach Publishers.

Paper, J. 1995. *The Spirits are Drunk: Comparative Approaches to Chinese Religion.* Albany: State University of New York Press.

Poo, M.-C. 1995. *Wine and Wine Offering in the Religion of Ancient Egypt.* London: Kegan Paul International.

Purcell, N. 1985. "Wine and Wealth in Ancient Italy." *The Journal of Roman Studies,* 75: 1–19.

Read B. E. n.d. *Chinese Materia Medica.* Shanghai: Henry Lester Institute for Medical Research.

Scheidel, W. and S. von Reden. 2002. *The Ancient Economy.* New York: Routledge.

Steele, P. 1994. *Food & Feast in Ancient Rome.* New York: New Discovery Books.

Tamang, J. P. 2010. *Himalayan Fermented Foods: Microbiology, Nutrition, and Ethnic Values.* New York: CRC Press, Taylor & Francis Group.

Valamoti, M. and M. Koukouli-Chrysanthaki. 2007. "Grape-pressings from northern Greece: the earliest wine in the Aegean." *Antiquity.* 81 (311): 54–61.

Wilson, H. 1988. *Egyptian Food and Drink.* Princes Risborough: Shire Publications.

2 Alcohol and the spread of culture in the Classical Period

In the Classical Period civilizations built upon previous accomplishments in order to form more developed societies and, in fact, empires. These empires spread across many parts of the world. Three empires exemplify the changes that took place during the Classical Period: the Mediterranean, China, and India. In each of these areas there began to be shared language and cultural values. The production, trade, consumption, and regulation of alcohol helped to shape the development of these consolidated civilizations. For example, the ceremonial production process of alcohol in China helped to define culture in that society. In the Mediterranean the trade of alcohol facilitated the spread of Greek and Roman culture. The consumption of alcohol in the Mediterranean, China, and India shaped class and gender roles as well as defined medicine, while the regulation of alcohol helped to moderate public behavior in all of those societies.

Classical Greece and the spread of the Roman Empire

Classical Greece rose after 800 BCE when small city states began to form around the Mediterranean. Roman civilization, which resembled Greek civilization, rose later, around 400 BCE and eventually spread as far as northern Africa and Britain. Alcohol production, trade, consumption, and regulation affected the development of the Greek and Roman civilizations. Production and trade of wine spread Greek and Roman culture across the Mediterranean and even into Africa, and pushed the Roman civilization as far as Britain. Consumption of wine solidified class as well as gender distinctions, and regulation of wine helped to develop social boundaries that came to define both civilizations. Finally, wine taxes remained necessary to support the governments as they continued to spread across the Mediterranean and beyond.

The production and trade of wine took place on the mainland of Greece as well as on the islands of Thasos, Lesbos, and Chios, all of which were known for producing high-quality wines. Grape growers planted vineyards close to waterways because shipping by water was much cheaper than overland shipping. By the beginnings of the Classical Greek civilization wine cultivation had developed into a much more complex process than in earlier periods. By that time, there was specialization within the profession of wine making and it had become one of the three most important trade items, alongside olives and grain. Greeks not only traded wine around the Mediterranean, but also spread its production to other parts of the Mediterranean as well, introducing wine making to parts of France and Italy. Moreover, Greek colonies established in Italy spread the knowledge of viniculture to the Romans. Wine not only brought the Romans Greek technology, but also Greek culture.

Romans also spread wine technology to the areas they dominated. Most of the wine produced in Rome came from large estates worked by slaves. These large estates continually developed new technologies. For example, in order to garner sweeter wines, wine makers left grapes in the sun for five to ten days, thus increasing the sugar content. Some wine makers left grapes on the vine (late harvest) in order to increase the sugar content and produce a sweeter wine. By the first-century CE Romans had developed over 91 varieties of wine, exemplifying the centrality of wine in Roman civilization. Romans spread wine technology to Gaul, Bordeaux, Provence, Languedoc, and finally to Burgundy and Alsace. Romans even produced wine in Britain, though the climate was not as conducive to wine growing as it was in parts of France. By disseminating wine technology, Rome was able to spread its culture throughout Europe.

The popularity of wine throughout the Greek and Roman Empires led to a vibrant trade in wine in the Mediterranean as well as to the overplanting of vineyards in some areas. For example, the founding of Marseille, a Phoenician colony, led to an intensification and diversification of the Mediterranean wine trade. During the fifth- and fourth-centuries BCE, Marseilles had a monopoly on the French wine trade. By the beginning of the first-century B.C.E., however, the Roman Empire had taken over the trade, as viticulture became a profitable business in Rome. Grape growing became even more intense after the eruption of Vesuvius in 79 CE, when not only Pompeii was covered by ash, but many vineyards were also. As a result, many vineyards were planted where wheat had been, eventually causing a shortfall of food and an edict from the emperor against planting any more vineyards. The intense trade in wine certainly helped to spread Roman civilization throughout the Mediterranean, while the choice to plant vineyards over even food demonstrated the critical role of wine not only in Roman culture but also in the economy.

The great Phoenician traders spread wine culture to northwest Africa which was agriculturally underdeveloped, having just emerged from the Neolithic age. During the Greco-Roman period (332 B.E–395 CE) the Phoenicians brought capital, technical expertise, and long-distance trading networks to the area, along with the domesticated grape. Cultivation of wine grapes began between the mid-fourth and the mid-second-centuries BCE. Because grapevines could be transported over long distances if kept moist and cool, the Phoenicians successfully started domestic viticulture in the Maghreb. The arrival of the Phoenicians drew the North Africans into the Mediterranean trading network through wine and thus into the advanced culture of the

Greco-Roman empire. As a result, social complexity followed trade, changing the social and cultural hierarchy of that area.

While production of wine in Greece and Rome clearly indicated its importance in each society, and trade in wine both expanded key trading networks and spread culture, the consumption of alcohol influenced Greece and Rome in even more ways. Consumption of beer and wine in Greek and Roman society helped to differentiate the elite from the lower class. Elite Greeks and Romans equated beer with the lower class. Beer was cheaper to make and was abundant. The majority of the populace consumed beer instead of water, likely because water was not clean. Moreover, beer was a part of daily nourishment for most Greeks, was used in offerings, and was buried with the dead to feed them in the next life. Poorer Greeks did drink wine, but of inferior quality, yet it was beer that structured their lives.

Wine consumption organized leisure, and defined culture, gender, and status. While Greeks of all classes drank wine, all Greek wine was not equal. Some scholars have argued that the ideas of equality in Greece led to the proliferation of wine consumption throughout society. Elites, however, drank the most expensive and high-quality wines as well as defined acceptable drinking habits across society. By the eighth to the sixth-century BCE, feasting and wine drinking were fully adopted into elite male society. Even Hippocrates said: "It is better to be full of wine than full of food." And in the Greek epics, *The Iliad* and *Odyssey*, wine and feasting were central to many parts of the stories.

Elite men drank wine on occasions called symposia. After dinner men gathered, lounged on couches, watched entertainment, and discussed politics. Many of these occasions included sex with prostitutes, young boys, or other men. The only women at these occasions were prostitutes or servants. Women's drinking was looked down upon by men, and women had the reputation of drinking to excess if allowed. Men also believed that women became promiscuous when they drank. Elite men also disapproved of the drinking habits of the lower classes. Moreover, elite drunkenness was acceptable, while drunkenness of the poor was criticized. Elites judged beer drinking or drinking undiluted wine to be uncivilized; both of which the lower classes did. Greeks believed that diluting wine, many times with three-quarters water, and drinking it in a proper setting, such as the symposia, was the only civilized way to imbibe. So while wine was available to all classes, consumption patterns structured elite male leisure, gender roles, social status, and the very definition of civilation.

Wine also shaped Greek medicine. Medical historian Salvatore Lucia wrote that physicians in the eighth and seven centuries BCE proclaimed that wine could cure fatigue, distress, pain, and sorrow, among other things. Moreover, Hippocrates wrote that wine could serve as an important additive to one's diet; it could be used as a dressing for a wound; and it could be used to calm fevers. He also wrote prolifically about the properties of various kinds of wines and how they affected the body. "Soft dark wines ... are flatulent and pass better by stool. Harsh white wines heat without drying, and they pass better by urine than by stool. New wines pass by stool better than other wines because they are ... more nourishing ... White wines and thin sweet wines pass better by urine than by stool ... but make the blood weak." (As quoted in Lucia, *A History of Wine as Therapy.*) Socrates, Plato, and Aristotle all wrote about the uses of wine both for medical purposes as well as for the general well-being of people.

In addition to shaping medicine, wine organized religious life in Greece. While wine accompanied most meals in Greece, it was only drunk after it was served to the god of wine, Dionysos. The Greeks held festivals called Dionysia, which were held in winter and spring. These festivals were full of drinking, dancing, and games, and people of all classes attended.

In Rome, drinking behavior was similar to that of Greece, as Romans also consumed prodigious amounts of wine. Wine consumption in Rome shaped elite leisure, daily sustenance, public socializing, medicine, and war. Elites held social events called convivium, much like the Greek symposia, where food and wine were served. Bars were also common in Rome, organizing the social lives of Romans. Wine punctuated Roman meals. Rod Phillips, a wine historian, argues that as the diet in Rome changed from porridge to bread, wine became necessary to wash down the dryer meal.

Romans also believed wine to be essential to health. One of the famous writers of the period, Aurelius Cornelius Celsus (25 BCE–37 CE) praised the health benefits of wine. He wrote that for stomach ailments, one should drink hot wine and then drink light and dry wine. In order to facilitate movement within the digestive tract one should drink sweet wine, and to slow down the digestive tract one should drink harsh or resinated wine. He also prescribed wine for nervous indigestion, jaundice, eye problems, ear problems, and various other maladies. In addition to Celsus, Pliny the Elder (23–79 CE) provided several remedies using wine. One such prescription for "beautiful and virtuous children", noted by Salvatore Lucia in his *History of Wine as Therapy*, called for "ground pine nuts, assorted fruits, honey, myrrh, saffron, yolk of egg, milk and palm wine." Another wine mixture was supposed to tame wild animals if sprinkled upon them. Yet another mixture of saffron and wine was used to alleviate itching and to help as a diuretic.

Moreover, wine was also mandated for the army. Wine, even if of inferior quality, was part of army rations. It was safer than water and soldiers expected to be able to imbibe. Some scholars argue that one of the reasons for the successes of the Roman army was that they carried wine as part of their rations, thus keeping their troops healthy – especially in siege conditions where potable water was extremely scarce.

As the Roman Empire spread into other areas, so did wine consumption habits. In the area of Anatolia wine had become an integral part of the diet by Classical Roman times, and several varieties existed. When the Romans invaded Britain, they created inns, called tabernae, where travelers could stop and imbibe along the roads that the Romans built. These tabernae changed the drinking environment of Britain. They increased wine drinking and acted as important purveyors of Roman culture.

As Christianity spread into Rome, it forever changed Roman culture as well as attitudes towards alcohol. Christianity began with the life of Christ in the Common Era and followed both the Old and New Testaments of the Bible. Like the Old Testament, the New Testament recommended the use of wine, although in moderation. Christians believed wine to be symbolic of Christ's blood, and therefore used it in important rituals. The New Testament section of the Bible both praised wine's benefits, and criticized its harmful effects. In I Timothy the Bible recommended the use of wine to alleviate illness. Jesus shared wine with his disciples at the ritual last supper. And in one of his most well-known miracles Jesus turned water into wine at a wedding feast. In another parable in the New Testament the Good Samaritan used wine and oil to treat the wounds of a Jewish victim he found along the road. While the New Testament lauded the moderate use of wine, it also warned against the excessive use of wine. For example in I Corinthians 11 it stated: "[do] not associate with any one who … is guilty of immorality or greed, or is an idolater, reviler, drunkard or robber," clearly equating drunkenness with other serious sins. The warnings against drunkenness came partly from the fear that Christians would partake in the pagan rituals in the cult of Dionysus, practiced by the Greeks, where drunkenness was common.

While wine consumption in Greek and Roman cultures shaped social status and identity, spread culture, and structured the growing Christian religion, the regulation of alcohol defined appropriate civic behavior based on age, status, occupation, and gender. Greek philosophers had much to say about the regulation of wine drinking. Some argued that when drunk in moderation wine was good for a person, it caused laughter and dancing, but it hurt men when drunk to intoxication. It could lead to crime, self-destruction, physical maladies, and the revealing of secrets. Both Philo and Plato agreed that a wise man could drink to excess periodically, as long as his behavior remained respectable. Philo went on to write, however, that temperance and sobriety were much better for both women and men, equating temperance and sobriety with a life of virtue. Plato, too, wrote that temperance on some occasions was very important. For example, he believed that one should only become intoxicated during festivals, but not during marriage ceremonies. He went on to argue that boys under 18 should not use wine at all, those in their twenties should use wine moderately, but those in their forties had the right to drink as much as they wanted. In Plato's final dialogue, *The Laws*, composed around 350 BCE, he outlined the public regulations of drinking in Carthage, which were not uniform across society, but based on one's station, helping to organize social mores in that city. He reported that regulations existed against drinking by soldiers on active duty, city magistrates and judges, ships' pilots, married couples intent upon procreation, all citizens during daytime hours, and all slaves, male or female, anytime.

Moreover, Roman regulations differed for men and women, perpetuating certain gender ideologies. Most women were not allowed to drink wine, and a man could divorce his wife if she became drunk without his knowledge. The

Roman philosopher Pliny the Elder loved wine, but thought women should not drink to excess. His view was shared by most. Some women were even killed by their families for drinking alcohol. Pliny said that the reason men kissed women upon greeting them was to see if they had been drinking alcohol. The rules about women drinking began to loosen around the end of the second-century BCE, however, when wine consumption rose in the general population.

Governments also taxed alcohol, seeing the opportunity to benefit from the high demand. In Plutarch's time, for example, some rulers destroyed personal vineyards in order to make sure that people secured a license to plant grapes. Wine was taxed during the Greco-Roman period (332 BCE–395 CE) in Africa. There were local customs duties and production taxes. The wine tax was to be paid in money, in contrast to earlier periods where it was paid in wine. The wine tax helped maintain and expand the government throughout the empire.

Classical China

During the Tang Dynasty China focused on building up the bureaucracy and the power of the emperor. Part of the construction of classical Chinese culture came from alcohol. Alcohol shaped culture through rituals and festivals, structured society by influencing social mores, and helped define the government's role in the civilization through regulations. When the Tang dynasty conquered Turfan in Central Asia, the most important tributes sent back were grapes and grape wine. The Tang then learned how to make grape wine. Even earlier than the Tang Dynasty, however, the Chinese both fermented and distilled alcohol. Some authors argue that the Chinese were the earliest to distill alcohol. Documents from 116 BCE, the books of Ssu Ma Ch-ien, and documents from 142 CE, the books of Wei Po Yang, appeared to show distillation information. Other authors argue, however, that distillation did not come to China until much later, in the twelfth-century.

The mandated ritualistic production of alcohol perpetuated its privileged place in Classical China. Records from about 500 CE described the proper way to ferment alcohol. Instructions from the Wei dynasty (386–534 CE) gave very specific directions. In August, workers, who had to be male, who were clean, and who had refrained from sex that day could make alcohol. They had to start with 50 liters of steamed, roasted, and raw wheat. A boy had to bring 1,000 liters of water, which no one else could touch. During the making of the alcohol the workers were directed to face west. First, the workers made the mixture of water and wheat into small cakes about two and a half inches in diameter and almost an inch thick. These cakes then dried in a sealed hut for seven days. Next, the workers turned the cakes over to dry for another seven days, after which they put them into a pile. They then took the cakes out of the hut, put them into a clay jar, and sealed the jar with mud to rest for another seven days. Next the workers made holes in the middle of the cakes and strung them up to dry in the sun. The cakes were most likely fermented with saliva. Finally, the workers pressed them with water.

The Chinese also made alcohol from fruit juice. Making alcohol from fruit juice was fairly simple, the fermentation process happened almost automatically if one left the juice alone to ferment. The sugar in the juice, combined with yeast, which could be found on the skins of fruits and in the dust of orchards and gardens, caused the fermentation process to take place.

Much like in the Mediterranean, alcohol consumption perpetuated certain social mores in China. For example, serving alcohol to guests was vital in China during the classical Han period, and hosts always served wine to their guests first, symbolizing respect and propriety. One story told of a man who sold his hair in order to afford alcohol for his guests. Moreover, wine also shaped high culture. Poets, calligraphers, and artists praised the ability of wine to bring out their best work. For example, the poet Wang Ji, of the Eight Immortals of the Wine Cup, wrote the poem: "In spring, pine needles ferment in the wine jugs; In autumn, chrysanthemums float in the wine cups. When we chance upon one another, we would rather get drunk, And definitely will not take up mixing the elixirs." (As quoted in McGovern, *Uncorking the Past.*) Another poet, Li Bai, who was very famous in the Tang Dynasty, wrote many of his poems about alcohol. Many believed that because most of his poems were about alcohol he wrote them while drunk.

Alcohol also figured prominently in festivals, shaping the activities. In the Festival of the Dead, which was two weeks after New Year, alcohol houses organized a parade that included the four levels of prostitutes. The parade also included guilds, merchants, and entertainers dressed as the Eight Immortals of Taoism. Other parade members carried jars of rice wine, which was much more popular than grape wine at that time.

In addition to urban rituals alcohol also structured rituals throughout the empire. Consumption rituals ushered in seasons, emphasized life changes, secured marriage alliances, and signified the arrival of peace across the empire. Alcohol was an important tool in peasant and noble rituals, and in solidifying political alliances. During spring festivals peasants drank prodigiously. Nobles, too, offered alcohol during their own elite ceremonies of passage. In addition, alcohol was central to rites of passage for young women and men. Offerings of alcohol from father to son consummated engagements between men and women. In other rituals, combatants offered a cup of alcohol to an enemy before battle, and after the battle the victors gave alcohol to the defeated. The victors then received the sacred cup of the ancestors. These rituals solidified the triumph of the winners and purged the enemy of the evil spirit that had possessed them to take to battle. After ritual tournaments, such as archery, the losers were offered cups of alcohol first and then afterward the winners drank. Drinking the cup signified the end of the battle and an oath against future attacks.

The Chinese regulated the use of wine and spirits, both legally and socially. For example, the emperor in 147 BCE, King Ti, "prohibited the preparation of certain alcoholic beverages." Around the same time period, one of the earliest Chinese medical texts, *Nei Ching*, from the Han Dynasty, about 200 BCE, warned against drinking at all, arguing it caused health as well as behavioral problems. Another famous precept stated: "The first glass, the man drinks the wine; the second glass, the wine drinks the wine; the third glass, the wine drinks the man." Buddhists banned alcohol, and some historians argue that the spread of Buddhism into China began to curb excessive drinking that had been a problem there in the pre-Buddhist period. Alcohol continued to have a profound effect on society, however, whether through its social and ritual use or through its regulation.

Classical India

During the later Vedic period in India, the highest caste, the Brahmins, led society. Alcohol helped shape many aspects of classical India, including medicine, society, culture, and religion. Indians created many kinds of alcohol. They drank Sura, a liquor made from fermented barley. Indians praised the drink, but also periodically condemned those who drank it. There was also an important drink called Soma, squeezed from a mountainous plant. A third drink during the Classical period was called parisruta and was prepared from fermented flowers or grasses. Fourth, there was a fermented rice drink made with spices. The production of so many kinds of alcohol ensured the influence of alcohol throughout Classical India.

Alcohol influenced the practice of medicine in Classical India. Many of the Classical writings in India showed alcohol to be central to medical cures. The Charaka Samhita, written between 600 BCE and 200 CE was part of the Ayur-Veda, an important Indian medical text. In this text wine was credited with helping with sleeplessness, sorrow, fatigue, digestion, and "cur[ing] the natural flow of internal fluids of the body." (As quoted in Lucia, *A History of Wine as Therapy*.) Later in the Tantras wine was worshipped for its powers to forget one's sorrows and to bring happiness. Buddhist and Jain literature prescribed alcohol to help with digestion, and Hindu literature prescribed wine as an anesthetic for medical operations. Wine was also used to heal animals. For example, wine was used in many remedies to heal elephants, which were sacred to the Hindus.

Alcoholic drinks constituted part of the diet of certain segments of Indian society, as prescribed by the Shastras, which were Hindu instruction books for living. The Tantriks, a group who countered the Vedas, promoted alcohol for medical reasons as well. Sushruta, a surgeon, who lived around the fourth-century BCE, stated that sura (an alcohol) should be used before a surgical operation as an anesthetic. Charak, a doctor, prescribed alcoholic drinks such as soma and sura as well as others to full-term pregnant women, and to women after the extraction of a dead fetus in order to ease pain.

Moreover, alcohol shaped Indian society. Many people consumed alcohol in taverns. These taverns were relatively large, contained many rooms, and some had beds. They were located mainly along trade routes and acted as inns for travelers. Women as well as men drank. It was less common for women, although Brahmin women were afforded more opportunities to embibe.

Alcohol also influenced the development of a major world religion that originated in India; Buddhism developed in India and centered around the teachings of the "enlightened one" or the Buddha. One of the five main precepts in Buddhism banned the use of alcohol. Early Buddhist literature especially forbade monks in monasteries from drinking alcohol. This literature also promoted asceticism, which dovetailed with the absence of alcohol. Despite Buddhist precepts, however, during the Buddhist period in India, around the fifth-century BCE, writings showed that drinking alcohol remained prevalent.

Many sacred texts included sections on the social regulation of alcohol. Many of these texts contradicted each other, however. The Smriti – a law code – stated that the higher castes should not drink wine. Another one of the most famous texts, the *Kama Sutra*, forbade wives from drinking wine, but allowed mistresses to drink wine. The two religious epics called *Ramayana* and the *Mahabharata* exalted wine as a drink for kings, sages, and hermits. Drinking alcohol, however, was one of the seven sins in the Vedas. Drinking was forbidden for Brahmins, elites, and students. In addition, a classic treatise on government, the *Arthashastra*, written by the prime minister under Maurya rule, argued that alcohol had disturbing effects, and forbade the use of it within the army. The government, however, also realized that alcohol taxes were so important to revenues, that curbing alcohol use would hurt the state and alcohol use continued to be widespread in Indian society.

Conclusion

Alcohol production and trade influenced all classical societies. Greece spread its culture into Rome through the wine trade. Subsequently, the spread of Greek and Roman viticulture and trade into newly conquered Northern Africa brought culture and social complexity into that region. Moreover, Romans spread their culture to Britain through the proliferation of tabernae along trade routes in that area. Similar to the Romans in Britain, in Classical India taverns existed along trade routes, which led to the expansion of Indian culture into other societies as well as the integration of other cultures into India. So the spread of alcohol into other civilizations in many cases led the way for the culture to follow.

Consumption of alcohol across civilizations influenced many areas of those societies such as medicine, religion, and class differentiation. First, consumption of alcohol helped to define medicine in many areas. Wine shaped the development of medicine in Greece and Rome as well as India, as it shaped classic treatises on health in all three cultures. Second, consumption of alcohol at religious and social festivals helped to define the belief systems in many cultures. For example, in Classical Greece, Rome, and China, alcohol was a primary ingredient in religious ceremonies and rituals.

Third, in many cultures the consumption of alcohol helped to differentiate among classes. Both Greek and Roman elites held banquets where drinking along with political and literary discussions took place, demonstrating their privileged positions in society. In China, alcohol characterized high culture because of its prominence in poetry and art, and in India the *Ramayana* and *Mahabharata* maintained that wine was for kings, while other treatises forbade Brahmins to drink, helping to define the culture of these segments in society.

Fourth, alcohol consumption influenced gender ideologies, especially surrounding women's sexuality. In Greek culture prostitutes were allowed to drink in the symposia, yet wives were prohibited because men equated women's alcohol use with promiscuous behavior. In China prostitution was associated with wine shops, and the Indian *Kama Sutra* allowed mistresses to drink.

Regulations of alcohol helped to form religions as well as to ensure the order of society. First, one of the five main precepts of Buddhism prohibited the use of alcohol; and while Christianity did not prohibit alcohol, it advocated for moderation. Second, alcohol regulation by the Greeks and Romans helped to keep order in the society through properly prescribing the appropriate relationship to alcohol based on occupation or gender. In Classical China alcohol was regulated in such a way as to instill the benefits of moderation in the populace.

Alcohol shaped many aspects of the world's Classical civilizations. Trade in alcohol brought culture along with it into many parts of the world. Use of alcohol shaped religion, class, and gender. And alcohol regulation influenced governments and religions in all these societies. Alcohol permeated the classical world, finding a place in the social, cultural, political, and economic realms in each society.

Further reading

Granet, M. 1958. *Chinese Civilizaation.* Trans. K. E. Innes and M. R. Brailsford. New York: Meridian Books, Inc.

Hewitt, T. F. 1980. *A Biblical Perspective on the Use and Abuse of Alcohol and Other Drugs.* Raleigh, NC: Pastoral Care Council on Alcohol and Drug Abuse.

Jennings, J., J. Jennings, K. L. Antrobus, S. J. Atencio, E. Glavich, R. Johnson, G. Loffler, and C. Luu. 2005. "Drinking Beer in a Blissful Mood: Alcohol Production, Operational Chains, and Feasting in the Ancient World." *Current Anthropology.* 46 (2): 275–303.

Lemu, B. A. 1992. *Islam and Alcohol.* Alexandria: Saadawi Publications.

O'Brian, J. M. and S. C. Seller. 1982. "Attributes of Alcohol in the Old Testament." *The Drinking and Drug Practices Surveyor.* 18: 18–24.

Prakash, O. 1961. *Food and Drinks in Ancient India: From Earliest Times to C. 1200 A.D.* Delhi: Munshi ram Manohar Lal.

Raymond, I. W. 1927. *The Teaching of the Early Church on the Use of Wine and Strong Drink.* New York: Columbia University Press.

Ssu-Hsieh, C. (of the later Wei Dynasty) 1945. Trans. H. Tzu-Ch'ing and C. Yünts'ung. "The Preparation of Ferments and Wines." *Harvard Journal of Asiatic Studies.* 9 (1): 24–44.

Waltham, C. (ed.) 1971. "Announcement About Drunkenness." In *ShuChing Book of History*, Chicago: Henry Regency Co.

3   Alcohol, cultural development, and the rise of trade in the Post-Classical and early modern world

Dramatic changes characterized many areas in the Post-Classical world. The rise of Islam and its spread across the Middle East and parts of Europe brought trade and technology in its wake. In the Americas vast empires expanded across the continent, creating sophisticated societies in Meso and South America. In the East modern forms of government and society began to develop, while in the West the growth of the merchant class and the rise of technology transformed society. The production, trade, consumption, and regulation of alcohol influenced many of these changes. For example, the production of alcohol in South America by women solidified gender roles in that area. Trade in alcohol across Western Europe facilitated the rising merchant class and the interactions among regions, while consumption patterns in Eastern Europe and Japan delineated social hierarchies in those areas. Finally, regulation of alcohol fostered the development of tax systems in Western Europe.

The Middle East

Islam began to define much of the Middle East toward the end of the Classical Period and beginning of the Post-Classical period. Arab Muslim armies conquered much of the Middle East, including parts of Africa and the Mediterranean. While the entire Middle East was not ethnically unified, Islam served to unite the area and provide the impetus for the spread of culture. Islam began in the 600s with the teachings of the prophet Muhammad, and soon spread throughout the Middle East and Asia. Alcohol regulation became one of the founding principles of the religion. Islam prohibited the consumption of alcohol. A perhaps apocryphal story explained why Mohammed believed drinking should not be tolerated in the Islamic religion. The story related that on one occasion when the prophet's disciples were drinking together, one of them from Mecca stood up and began to recite a rather uncomplimentary poem about one of the disciples from Medina. This resulted in the recipient of the poem hurling a bone at the head of the reciter. Mohammed supposedly asked God, Allah, how to remedy such problems. The result was that alcohol should be outlawed in the religion. Historians have argued that refraining from alcohol was a way for Muslims to distinguish themselves from the Christians who drank wine.

In any event, the spread of Islam across the Middle East and North Africa dramatically decreased alcohol consumption in those areas, but it did not completely erase it. Religious proponents destroyed many vineyards and thus wine consumption necessarily diminished. Sometimes, however, non-Muslims in a religious area were allowed to continue to brew and consume alcohol. And there were still poems that extolled the virtues of wine. In addition, a Persian tradition, for example, allowed for moderate consumption of wine if one was ill. There were other ways around the prohibition of wine by Islam as well. For example, boiling wine or adding salt or relishes to it made it acceptable to drink.

The Quran also mentioned that there were some benefits from wine, and Mohammed claimed that for those Muslims who made it to heaven, wine would be part of the reward. Islamic physicians also used wine to cure ills. One prominent Persian physician, Avicenna (980–1036 CE) wrote that white wine could relieve headaches, and that wine was good for digestion. At the same time, however, he wrote that children should not be given wine and that frequent intoxication was bad for the body, particularly the liver, brain, and nerves. The Quran also noted that wine caused more ills than benefits. Early portions of the Quran mentioned that it was impossible to meditate or pray while intoxicated. Later verses stated that there was a link between wine and a variety of social evils.

Some scholars have argued that the prohibition of wine in the Quran was ambiguous, and that it was not the use of wine, per se, but the use of wine in pagan rituals that was outlawed. Other scholars have argued that rather than being explicitly forbidden like blood or pork or carrion, the Quran maintained that it was the misuse of alcohol that caused severe social problems. It could create divisions among men, and could separate them from God. These historians contend that the prohibition of wine came more from a historical context than divine law. Theocrats in Muslim countries during Mohammed's time did enact controls to regulate drinking. Group pressure was used to curb drinking, and under subsequent caliphates punishments for drinking ranged from between 40 and 80 lashes.

Indeed as Islam spread across parts of the Middle East, Northern Africa, and Europe it changed the drinking habits of the societies there. The absence of alcohol brought on by Islam changed the nature of rituals and ceremonies, as well as social interactions in those cultures. In some regions abstinence did not prevail, however. For example, in Spain wine drinking continued, even in Muslim societies. Similar to the famous symposia of the Greeks, men gathered in the evening and drank, talked, and read poetry. So even in Islam many contradictions existed between the precepts and actual practice. It can be said, however, that the prohibition of alcohol considerably shaped the cultures to which it spread.

Pre-colonial Americas

In the Americas during the pre-colonial period, large sedentary populations grew in Meso-America and in the Andes. Each had their own kind of alcohol based upon the plants available to them. Mexicans drank pulque, made from the agave plant, and Andeans drank chicha, made from corn. In each civilization alcohol figured prominently in daily life, as well as in the cultural construction of gender, social hierarchy, and religion. Alcohol production, consumption, and regulation in the Americas helped define the Aztec and Inca empires. In Meso-America the ubiquity of pulque, even with its long and intense production process, suggests how important alcohol was to that society. The Aztecs regulated its consumption, helping to solidify class and gender distinctions within the empire, and reinforcing the control of the state over its people. Since pulque was consumed during most ritual and ceremonial occasions it helped to define social and religious structures within the empire as well. In Peru, chicha, much like pulque, was important to ceremonies in the Inca empire. Only women produced chicha, so chicha production helped to define gender roles in that culture. Inca leaders regulated chicha use, which became an important tool to strengthen the control of the empire over its conquered areas. In these ways alcohol was central to the development of class, gender, and governmental control in both cultures.

In Mexico, alcohol, in this case pulque, shaped history and religion. According to one folktale, pulque was discovered by a great Toltec noble named Papantzin. Evidence suggest, however, that it was likely used at least 1,500 years before the Toltec civilization. From as early as 200 CE stone carvings showed pulque, although no evidence exists regarding the beginnings of its production. Aztec society linked pulque with fertility, femininity, and agriculture; the goddess of pulque, Mayahuel, was an earth mother who had 400 breasts.

The production of pulque required several years and was very involved. The maguey plant, which was a type of agave plant similar to a cactus, had to grow for eight to ten years in order to mature enough to make pulque. After the plant matured the juice of the plant was extracted over a period of months and stored inside containers inside a tinacal, which was a special building made for that purpose. Pulque was also made by removing the leaves from the agave to get to the heart of the plant. Workers cut the heart into two pieces and slow-cooked it for two or three days in a below-ground earthen oven lined with moist leaves of the plant. Afterwards, the hearts were removed and laid in the sun for several days to dry. After the hearts dried, the pulp was separated from the fiber, and then steeped in water to begin fermentation. The name pulque in Nahuatl means decomposed, or spoiled, which probably relates to the fact that it did not keep long, sometimes only a day after being made.

Consumption patterns of pulque during the Aztec period shaped religion, ritual, social status, and medicine. The Aztecs predominantly used pulque for ritual and medicinal purposes. Only during designated annual ceremonies were people allowed to be publicly intoxicated. For example, annual feasts in honor of the gods as well as harvest festivals called for mass drinking. William Taylor points out in *Drinking, Homicide, and Rebellion in Colonial Mexican*

Villages that other occasions for drinking in pre-colonial Mexico included births, weddings, funerals, and a warrior's rights of passage, all of which justified several days of drinking. During all other times of the year only elites, the elderly, and people who were considered wise were allowed to drink pulque. The majority of the population was rarely allowed to drink. Lower-class women could drink pulque after giving birth, men could drink after strenuous work, and warriors were given pulque after a victory. Drinking pulque on these occasions was allowed because pulque was thought to restore strength. In order to regulate the use of pulque Aztec leaders imposed several punishments for casual pulque drinking, which ranged from having one's head shaved in public, to whipping, or even stoning. These regulations in Aztec society emphasized who could drink and when they could drink, but not how much. Excessive drinking during sanctioned occasions was expected. Taylor points out that "[p]ulque, then, was an important drink … before the conquest: not really a forbidden drink, but a powerful, almost sacred substance, with unpredictable effects, and generally controlled by rules of periodic, ritual use." Pulque held an important place in the religion and society of the Aztecs and was central in defining how festivals and rituals took place.

In Peru, the first evidence of chicha comes from the period 500–300 BCE. Chicha was generally made from maize, but it could also be made from quinoa, manioc, and peanuts – depending upon the region. The most common kind of chicha was maize chicha, however. Chicha was used in the pre-Incaic empire of the Chimu Indians of Peru. People in that society drank chicha every day as a food-beverage and also used it during ceremonial occasions as well as work parties. Both individual households as well as political leaders used chicha to gather workers.

During the Inca period chicha influenced origin myths, gender idologies, religion, and the spread of culture. The origin myths of the Inca state included chicha. The Incas believed that the four ancestors of the Incas came out of three caves in a mountain called Tambo T'oco. Manco Capac, one of the four men from the mountain, pulled out some corn seeds that he had brought from the cave where he had emerged and then planted the first cornfield in the Cusco valley. Chicha then began to be made from that field. In another myth, Mama Huaco, one of the original ancestors, planted the first field of corn. After she died her body was embalmed and mummified and the people responsible for caring for her mummy made chicha from the corn grown in that field. The chicha was given to those who maintained her cult.

Only women produced chicha, providing a key component in the makeup of female gender identity. Specially chosen women, called mamacona, made chicha for the Inca king. These women were judged the most beautiful in the kingdom and were required to be virgins. They were revered and lived their lives in large, state-run centers made especially for producing chicha and weaving cloth. They procured their grain from tribute to the king and thus had a never-ending supply of maize for their work. Not only did mamacona make chicha for the kingdom, but also individual women made chicha in their homes. Chicha production began when women shaped mouth-sized balls of maize dough and masticated these dough balls until sugar was produced from the starch. To cook the chicha women used large clay pots over open fire pits. A woman heated water in one pot and then poured that hot water over the masticated maize in another clay pot. She then stirred the mixture until it became a paste, which took several hours. The paste slowly separated into liquid at the top and solids at the bottom. Then she boiled more water and slowly added this water to the mixture of masticated corn and water until it produced a cloudy mixture, which she stirred into a soupy consistency. After the mixture rested it separated into three layers. The top layer was skimmed off into a separate pot, as was the second layer. These two layers became chicha after a few days of fermentation. Chicha was opaque and effervescent and tasted a little like apple cider. It usually contained less than 5 percent alcohol, although it could contain up to 12 percent alcohol. Chicha was drunk through straws put into various drinking vessels shaped into llama heads, reed boats, and even the skulls of enemies, all of which held meaning for the Incas.

Chicha also structured the daily lives of the Incas, shaped religious and social ceremonies, and spread Inca culture throughout the empire. Most Andeans in corn-producing areas drank chicha as one of their main food sources. It contained numerous vitamins and nutrients. Inca leaders and their subordinates drank chicha during major feasts and work parties. It was also used in ceremonies of large land holders (patrons) and their workers. Moreover, Incan kings offered chicha to their gods and ancestors. Patrick McGovern in *Uncorking the Past* describes how in a ritual the king poured chicha into a golden bowl located on a throne in the central plaza of the capital. The chicha spilled down the "gullet of the Sun God" into the Temple of the Sun. In addition, commoners drank prodigious amounts of chicha during festivals. Moreover, human sacrifices were "rubbed in the dregs of chicha and then tube-fed with more chicha for days while lying buried alive in tombs." Some authors argue that maize chicha was also crucial in the spread of Incan culture throughout the empire. For example, Inca chiefs gave villagers in far-flung regions of the empire abundant chicha to drink at large banquets held to reinforce the power of the chief. In addition, when Inca representatives stopped along the roads as they traveled, people expected them to provide chicha. In return, the Inca received both the loyalty and the work of the villagers in the Inca's fields. It therefore was the most important piece of material culture that represented and reinforced the social and political hierarchy within the Inca state.

Post-Classical and early-modern Eastern Europe

In Post-Classical and early modern Eastern Europe alcohol swayed the course of religion, defined social status, and structured festivals. When in the tenth-century one Russian state, led by Vladimir, began to move toward a central religion, alcohol shaped the decision. Alcohol was so important in Russian society that Vladimir rejected Islam, for example, because of its proscription against alcohol. The most popular alcoholic drinks in Russia were kvas, which was a rye-based beer, and mead. Elites drank mead, especially in the thirteenth-century when its main ingredient, honey, grew scarce because the bee population died out. As in other areas of Europe, elites also drank wine. Wine was imported to Poland, especially the city of Cracow, which was a trade hub. From here wine was transported to other Eastern European areas and to the Baltic region. The consumption of mead and wine, then, became a way for elites to culturally separate themselves from the rest of the population in early modern Russia and other parts of Eastern Europe.

Peasants drank beer. As in other agricultural societies drinking was a social ritual, based on the agricultural calendar. Binge, or excessive drinking took place during harvest time. Brewing beer was so important to the peasant class, in fact, that even in the times of famine, especially the great famine of 1601, beer brewing continued. Heavy alcohol consumption continued to be emblematic of Russian society throughout the modern period.

Post-Classical and early-modern Japan

Alcohol trade and consumption significantly influenced the development of Japan. During the Heian period, between 794 and 1185 the royal court focused on ultra-polite behavior and luxury. Part of the aristocratic lifestyle was the use of sake, or rice wine, which began to be produced in this period. Political leaders controlled the production of sake, and the royal court designated court brewers to make sake for ritual use. Because it was controlled by royalty and elites, access to sake was one of the factors that effectively separated the classes. Sake production continued to develop between 1185 and 1573, when the court, or shogunate, allowed select families to start independent breweries. These brewing families sold sake at the gates to the temples on market days and competed with each other for customers. Sake became an important commodity, which influenced the development of commercialization in Japan. Ceremonial use of sake helped to structure rituals in early modern Japan. For example, in rural areas most drinking took place during big celebrations where the community made large amounts of alcohol and drank it for days until it was finished. Alcohol continued to shape the Japanese economy and culture as Japan advanced into the modern world.

Post-Classical and early modern West

The West underwent many changes during the Middle Ages and the early modern periods. Improvements in agriculture, expansion of trade, and a rise in technology characterized these periods. Moreover, between the tenth and thirteenth-centuries population levels rose, adding to urbanization. The production, trade, consumption, and regulation of alcohol especially helped to influence the rise and regulation of trade, as well as to shape gender roles, religious practices, and the rules of civic society in Western civilization during the centuries that ushered in the modern world.

Production of wine in Britain increased early in the Post-Classical period. With the introduction of Christianity in Britain in the sixth-century, monasteries proliferated. These monasteries frequently had large vineyards and produced wine and other alcohols. The monasteries made money from the vineyards by renting them out and being paid in wine. The monks also used the wine for prescriptions as the monasteries sometimes became hospitals for the sick. Moreover, monasteries also spread throughout Western Europe creating vineyards as they went, and, as a result, viticulture and viniculture helped solidify the presence of Christianity across Europe.

Not only was wine important in the monasteries, but it also played a major role in accelerating long-distance trade. With the population boom in Europe after 1000 CE elites demanded luxury goods and wine was one of the important luxury items they demanded. The nobility, higher clergy, and wealthier townspeople had a taste for wines. For example, it was not unusual for aristocratic households to spend 30 to 40 percent of their budget on wine. Therefore, from places such as Bordeaux, where vines became more numerous, wine was shipped out to England. French wine tended to last no more than a year and therefore more stable wines from Greece and Italy were also shipped to England. By the early fourteenth-century, wine represented more than 30 percent of English imports and 25 percent of all imports to the Low Countries. The growing demand for wine greatly stimulated commercial viticulture in France, Italy, Spain, Greece, the Mediterranean islands, and parts of Germany. It also led to commercial as well as technological advancements in the industry. In order to facilitate trade, vintners often organized into guilds and imported wine wholesale. In some towns they also monopolized the retail sale of wine, but in general, growing numbers of taverns controlled most of the direct sale of wine to the consumer. This period of increased demand also resulted in technological advancement. Larger wine presses came into use and the technology of growing grapes developed. Viticulturalists began to take greater care in cultivation by loosening the soil around the vines for better water absorption and removing unnecessary leaves to increase yield. Wine, then, helped to intensify long-distance trade throughout Europe as well as to shape elite identity and culture in the early modern period.

While wine was sold to the elite, ale was sold to common people. Ale, made from malted barley, water, and yeast, was the staple drink of the vast majority of those who lived in England, the Low Countries, Scandinavia, northern France, and much of Germany and Eastern Europe. Unlike wine, however, ale was considered a food necessity, not a luxury drink, and it structured the daily diets of most Europeans. Moreover, brewing ale was a household industry, especially in rural areas, and was considered the purview of women. So by the fourteenth-century the majority of those selling ale were women, helping to define female identity during that period. Interestingly, most of the ale traders came from middling to upper-class families. Some poorer women sold ale as well, but usually did not stay in the trade very long, only selling ale when they were in dire straights. The elite female ale sellers, however, remained in their occupation for several years, most more than a decade. Even so, they did not sell ale year round. Rather, ale shops only opened when harvests supplied the grain to women to make ale.

Trade of ale by women continued to spread in the Post-Classical and early modern periods. Brewers sold their ale through alehouses, purchasing their supplies from commercial brewers. Alehouses in rural areas were often extensions of homes, too small to house many people; it was more common for customers to bring in their pail and carry the purchased ale back home to consume. Brewers placed stakes or other signs outside their houses when they had prepared a fresh batch of ale. They also had to display a bush or bunch of ivy on the end of the stake so the local ale-tasting officials knew they could now come to evaluate and price the ale.

In urban areas the establishments were larger and sold ale more consistently. In general, more formal alehouses took shape between the twelfth and the fifteenth-centuries and the quality of the ale improved over that time as well. Before the plague of the fourteenth-century most of the alehouses were transitory in nature. As a result of the plague, however, the trade in ale changed. More people were able to buy ale because wages rose. At the same time, the poorer women who periodically sold ale were not forced into that occupation, so the number of sellers decreased and the occupation became more professionalized. By the 1400s alehouses sometimes provided lodging, food, and entertainment. By the sixteenth-century 86 percent of the drinking establishments in England were alehouses. Even though alehouses were very popular they produced small amounts of ale, and quality still varied from house to house. Ale spoiled within five days or so, thus it had to be brewed quite frequently, and as a result was not a very profitable business. The legally fixed price of ale remained the same from the thirteenth up to the sixteenth-century, even though brewers continually tried to get the price raised.

Tremendous changes took place in the business of fermented grains in the early modern period. The Dutch created hopped beer in the fifteenth-century, so beer made from malt, hops, and water became increasingly popular, eclipsing ale, especially in Holland and Germany. Hopped beer was weaker, more bitter, and less perishable than ale. It was also easier to make in large quantities, and thus more profitable. The addition of hops to ale acted as a preservative; beer brewers could trade their product over longer distances and thus could become highly commercialized.

Hopped beer was brewed and traded by men, which led to identifying the industry as masculine, effectively marginalizing ale women and modifying gender ideologies in early modern Europe. These male beer brewers organized into guilds, unlike alewives who rarely did so. By the sixteenth-century there were large, male-dominated breweries in the city of London. These large breweries began to make huge profits trading beer internationally, opening new markets for European trade. For example, breweries sold beer to Russia in exchange for imported Russian goods that were then sold at higher prices in England. India, too, became a destination for British beer. The international beer industry, then, solidified beer as one of Britain's signature trade items.

An even more monumental change occurred in alcohol production in the early modern period. The process of distilling alcohol (as opposed to the chemical distillation of many other substances) "profoundly influenced the art of distilling" according to R. J. Forbes in *Short History of the Art of Distillation*. Distillers were often connected to vintners or beer makers. Distilling was thought of as a fine art, and distillers kept their recipes very secret. Distilled spirits began to be produced in the West during the early modern period as well. Some historians argue that the Arabs discovered distillation around the tenth-century CE, while others argue that the Chinese discovered them much earlier. Still others argue that distillation began when the Scottish distilled mead in the sixth-century. Distilled alcohol was made from fermented grains, potatoes, and fruits, among other things. Spirits were made in a still, which was an enclosed vessel. It had to have a fire underneath it to start the process. The idea was to separate the liquor (which boiled at 173 degrees Fahrenheit) from water (which boiled at 212 degrees Fahrenheit). The alcohol became vapor and then moved to a final container through a vapor line. As it cooled down, it became a more concentrated liquid, or distilled spirits.

Alcohol made from the distillation of corn in the Low Countries, England, and northern Germany began to compete with wine, which remained expensive. Italian distillers brought liqueurs to Paris as early as 1332. These liqueurs were popular among the wealthy, who expressed their elite culture through its consumption. Distillation spread as far north as Scandinavia. The Dutch, however, were the ones who began to trade distilled alcohol throughout Western Europe. One of the first kinds of distilled wine, brandy, became very popular in Western Europe, bolstering the commercial status of the Dutch who traded it.

As the production of distilled liquor began to spread, more types of spirits were created. In areas where grain rather than grapes grew, beer was distilled into whiskey. Scotland became known for the distillation of whiskey beginning in about the fifteenth-century. In England, gin, flavored with juniper berries, became a popular drink in the slums of London. Much of the distilled liquor in England and Holland was flavored with spices like rosemary, sandalwood, basil, ginger, and cardamom. Both England and Holland were engaged in the spice trade, and so they procured spices from abroad and then used them to flavor the new spirits.

Consumption of wine, ale, beer, and spirits profoundly shaped Western Europe. Wine consumption characterized class identity in many areas in Europe. Wine was the most popular drink of the upper classes, becoming identified with that segment of society. When the middling classes began to gain wealth as a result of commercial development, they strove to emulate elite culture. One of the most easily attainable and observable ways to do so was to drink wine. Moreover, because it was a luxury item it became a favored reward for those who worked for the elite. Artisans as well as laborers received some wine as part of their pay from the elites for whom they worked. Soldiers, too, received a portion of wine as part of their rations.

A majority of the people in the Post-Classical and early modern period consumed ale, however, as it continued to be a very important ingredient in their daily lives. For example, ale was popular at church events. Churches in the thirteenth- and fourteenth-centuries had ale parties to raise money. Villagers made ale, brought it to the function, and the profits went to the church. The leftover ale from the two or three day party went to any of the village bachelors who could still stand. Weddings and funerals always provided ale for the attendees; hundreds of gallons of ale were drunk at these events. Just like in the earlier part of the Post-Classical period, then, alcohol was associated with the church.

People also consumed ale in alehouses. Alehouses were centers of gossip, as well as places where people came to socialize, conduct business, and to discuss literature, art, and politics. As trade increased in Britain, those doing business in urban areas increasingly used alehouses (along with taverns and inns) for business meetings. Members of guilds organized social events in alehouses, and some alehouses became the centers of political activities, housing political clubs. Ale houses or pubs also hosted large celebrations such as baptisms, funerals, and wakes. In addition, brewers made special ales for events and celebrations, naming their batches marriage ale, childbirth ale, journey ale, or Christmas ale.

Ale was still relatively expensive for workers to consume, however. A gallon of ale in the thirteenth-century cost a laborer two-thirds of his daily wages and a craftsman one-third of his daily wages. Poor laborers had access to ale because many landlords included some ale in their wages. And soldiers had access to ale through drink rations. The plague in the fourteenth-century, however, allowed more people access to ale. Because of the decline in the number of laborers, demand for laborers increased and thus wages increased. With rising wages laborers could afford about three times as much ale in 1400 as they could in 1300. By the fifteenth- and sixteenth-centuries, however, hopped beer and gin surpassed ale in popularity with the working classes.

Society continued to believe in the curative properties of alcohol. Apothecaries commonly prescribed beer and spirits to their patients. Moreover, doctors began to prescribe spirits for various illnesses such as diarrhea and typhoid fever, accelerating the spread of spirits across Western Europe in the early modern period. In the sixteenth- and seventeenth-centuries beer was considered a cure for many illnesses. For example, buttered beer was supposed to cure coughs and shortness of breath; and other beers were supposed to cure gout and consumption; and yet another beer, along with other drugs, was used as an anesthetic.

In addition to production, trade, and consumption of alcohol, the regulation of alcohol had an impact on the development of a commercial culture, social development, and government stability in the Post-Classical and early-modern West. Strict regulations controlled the price and quality of wine. In

1330 the London authorities, for example, fixed the price of different qualities of wine; a gallon of the best Gascon wine could sell for no more than four pence, while a gallon of Rhine wine could retail for up to eight pence. In the provinces authorities allowed slightly higher prices in order to cover the costs of transportation. Unfortunately, prices were difficult to enforce, especially during the Hundred Years War, which caused frequent interruptions in supply. Alcohol was not only regulated by the government, but also by the guilds. The Vintner's Company, which was a guild of wine merchants in London, controlled both the wholesale and retail wine trade. The group mandated that wines could only be unloaded off ships by specific workmen, and sold to taverns only in wholesale. The Vintners' Guild also controlled the retail sale of the wine. Many of the regulations by the guilds aimed to keep the quality of wine high. The government also levied taxes on wine, which significantly strengthened the treasury of the crown. Taxes were paid in currency as well as in kind, therefore securing more wine for the royal household.

Much like wine, the price, quality, and measurement of ale were strictly regulated. In England, the government fixed the price of ale based on the changing price of grain from which malt was made. Similar regulations were in force elsewhere in Europe by town decree. Laws limited the price an alewife could ask; if she charged too much she had to pay fines. The quality of ale was regulated by ale tasters, who were appointed or elected in every town and village. Brewers who used impure water or bad malt, who sold ale before the dregs settled or when it was old and spoiled, or who tried to pass off weak ale as a more expensive grade were fined by the local authorities. The measurement of ale was regulated as well. Abuses were frequent, however. Brewers put false bottoms in their measures or used elaborately shaped vessels that held less than the designated amount of ale. As a result, these laws were difficult to enforce. Most brewers found it more profitable to break the laws and pay the fines. By the late medieval period most alewives were paying "pre-emptive" fines to the court for selling ale. These pre-emptive fines eventually became licensing fees charged by the lords.

Governments not only regulated trade and levied taxes, but they also regulated consumption. Expansion of trade in distilled spirits, especially gin, brought about stricter laws aimed to curb drinking spirits in general. Most of the severe problems of drunkenness were associated with spirits. Public drunkenness was punishable in many parts of Europe, setting social standards for a growing European population. In Frankfurt, laws were passed as early as 1360 to regulate the consumption of brandy. Town councils all over Europe raised taxes on spirits as an attempt to curb their appeal. The town of Nürnberg put forth the following edict in 1496. "As many persons in this town have appreciably abused drinking aquavit the town council warns earnestly and they stress that from now on Sundays or other official holidays no spirit shall be kept in the houses, booths, shops or market and even the streets of this town for the purpose of sale or paid consumption." (As quoted in Forbes, *Short History of the Art of Distillation.*) Regulation of alcohol strengthened the role of government in the development of trade, as well as in the development of social mores in the Post-Classical and early modern periods.

Conclusion

Alcohol production, trade, consumption, and regulation changed dramatically over the Post-Classical and early-modern periods, affecting societies in new ways. The production and trade of alcohol influenced gender roles and the spread of culture in several ways. First, the production of alcohol exclusively by one sex helped to distinguish gender roles within societies. For example, inside the Inca Empire making chicha was the exclusive purview of women, categorizing it as feminine. In Britain in the Middle Ages women made and sold ale, idealizing that trade as feminine. Then in the early-modern period in Britain, as beer overtook ale, men stepped into the beer business, excluding women and creating an occupation that became identified as masculine.

Consumption of alcohol shaped many aspects of Post-Classical and early modern societies, including medicine, religion, and class. First, across widely disparate cultures alcohol shaped medicine. Islamic doctors prescribed alcohol, believing in its healing powers, even with the religious edict against its use. Aztec doctor/priests also ordered alcohol for the sick, as that society believed in its curative powers as well. Additionally, in the sixteenth- and seventeenth-century British apothecaries and doctors prepared their medicines using beer and spirits as ingredients. Second, use of alcohol at religious rituals and social festivals helped to define belief systems and mark important events in virtually every culture. The ceremonies of the Incas, Aztecs, Russians, Japanese, and British all featured alcohol. Conversely, yet equally as important, the ban on the use of alcohol in Islam shaped that belief system.

Third, in many cultures alcohol consumption patterns helped to define class identity. In Post-Classical Russia mead and wine characterized elite culture, while kvas beer characterized peasant identity. Alcohol use signified status in Post-Classical Japan where elites drank sake, and in Post-Classical and early modern Britain where elites drank wine and brandy, while commoners drank ale, and later beer and gin. In Aztec society elites had the privilege of drinking alcohol at any time, while commoners could only drink on special or ritual occasions, creating distinct differences between the two groups.

Regulation of alcohol provided governments with a way to control society as well as commerce. The Aztecs strictly regulated alcohol in order to maintain social hierarchy and public order. Islamic governments forbade alcohol as a way to strengthen Muslim identity. The government in early modern Britain regulated alcohol to bring standards to the alcohol business in a growing commercial economy. The British government also regulated the use of spirits to keep public order, especially aimed toward the lower class. Almost universally across cultures, alcohol regulation acted as a particularly invasive way to control the populace, mainly the lower class.

In the Post-Classical and early modern periods production and trade of alcohol spread culture and helped to define gender roles; consumption of alcohol helped to define medicine, class, and gender across many civilizations; and regulation of alcohol strengthened social hierarchy, commerce, and religious identity. In essence, alcohol touched virtually every segment of society, shaping the lives of people in countless ways.

Further reading

Bennett, J. M. 1996. *Ale, Beer, and Brewsters in England: Women's Work in a Changing World, 1300–1600.* New York: Oxford University Press.
Berger, P. 1985. *The Art of Wine in East Asia.* San Francisco: Asian Art Museum of San Francisco.
Bruman, H. J. 2000. *Alcohol in Ancient Mexico.* Salt Lake City: University of Utah Press.
Clark, P. 1983. *The English Alehouse: a Social History, 1200–1830.* New York: Longman.
Forbes, R. J. 1948. *Short History of the Art of Distillation: from the Beginnings up to the Death of Cellier Blumenthal.* Leiden: E.J. Brill.
Hackwood, F. W. 1985. *Inns, Ales and Drinking Customs of Old England.* London: Bracken Books.
Jennings, J. 2005. "La Chichera y El Patrón: Chicha and the Energetics of Feasting in the Prehistoric Andes." In *Archaeological Papers of the American Anthropological Association.* 14: 241–59.
Lucia, S. P. M. D. 1963. *A History of Wine As Therapy.* Philadelphia: J. B. Lippincott Company.
Martin, A. L. 2001. *Alcohol, Sex, and Gender in Late Medieval and Early Modern Europe.* New York: Palgrave (St. Martins).
McGovern, P. E. 2009. *Uncorking the Past: The Quest for Wine, Beer and Other Alcoholic Beverages.* Berkeley, CA: University of California Press.
Moore, J. D. 1989. "Pre-Hispanic Beer in Coastal Peru: Technology and Social Context of Prehistoric Production." *American Anthropologist* 91 (3): 682–95.
Scholliers, P. (ed.) 2001. *Food, Drink and Identity: Cooking, Eating and Drinking in Europe Since the Middle Ages.* New York: Berg.
Watney, J. 1974. *Beer is Best: A History of Beer.* London: Peter Owen.

4 Colonizers and the colonized

Alcohol in the fifteenth- through the nineteenth-centuries

In the 400 years between the 1400s and 1800s two world trends emerged. A world economic system developed, which went hand in hand with European colonization. Called the Atlantic world system by many scholars, the economic structure encompassed multiple continents. Europeans introduced an expanded and intensified market economy. The trade included a variety of goods, and a significant trade good was alcohol. Alcohol played a role in the expanding economies as a sought after commodity and sometimes as currency itself. Several European countries relied on alcohol to pay for hundreds of thousands of slaves from West Africa. The trade in alcohol rather than its production, consumption, or regulation dominated its story in these centuries.

In the other world trend in this period, colonization, the story of alcohol differed. Its production, trade, consumption, and regulation influenced the European colonies and their development. Indigenous demand for alcohol aided in the colonization of North America and Latin America. Alcohol influenced the economic and cultural development of the colonies and new kinds of alcohol, especially distilled liquor, substantially changed the lives of indigenous North Americans and Latin Americans.

European trade

The alcohol trade significantly influenced the growth of the world economic system in the early modern period. European countries earned tremendous profits from the trade. Alcohol was shipped throughout Europe, used aboard ships, and sold to the New World in exchange for everything from timber to slaves. Spain, for example, through exploiting its colonies for silver, was able to inflate the price of wine and earn enormous profits, adding to its already prosperous position. The Portuguese also shipped substantial amounts of alcohol throughout Europe, India, Africa, and the Americas, making them competitive in world trade. Moreover, the promise of alcohol on the arduous voyages successfully enticed Portuguese sailors to board ships. The Dutch traders also relied on alcohol. Like Portugal, the Netherlands plied its sailors with liquor. The Dutch shipped brandy throughout Europe, increasing alcohol consumption in many areas. The French, too, with wine, made significant inroads into international trade. French wine became so well known that people began to identify certain varieties with elites, and other varieties with the lower classes, giving French wine the ability to characterize social status, an ability that has lasted into the twenty-first-century.

In the fifteenth-century Western Europe started exploring and constructed a complex trading and colonial system that would change the face of the globe. The path to exploration had been left open for the Western Europeans by the Chinese, who even though they had had naval and maritime superiority in the fourteenth-century, ceased their movement into trade expansion and instead focused solely on Southeast Asia. Moreover, the breakdown of the Middle-Eastern Caliphates meant that the Middle East was not in a position to begin costly and risky exploration into the unknown.

The Atlantic system, led by European traders, became the center of much of the global trade. And alcohol became one of the important trade goods throughout Europe and from Europe to Africa, North America, and Latin America. Wine as well as distilled liquors were exported throughout the Atlantic system. Countries such as Spain, Portugal, the Netherlands, and France all participated in the trade. Alcohol helped the growth of the economies of these as well as other European countries. Many of these states had a monopoly on the liquor trade and auctioned off the right to distill, produce, and trade alcohol. The winners of the alcohol auctions made sizeable profits in the trade, and each state made considerable profit as well.

During the expansion of world trade Spain exported increasing amounts of wine to Europe as well as to the New World. Part of the reason for Spain's success in the wine trade came from inflation caused by the influx of silver from Spain's Latin American colonies. Inflation brought an increase in the price of Spain's wine and caused a rush to plant vineyards because of the chance to make extraordinary profits from the trade. The wine trade considerably boosted the economy of Spain during the colonial period.

Portugal, too, carried substantial quantities of grape wine on its trading and exploratory ships during colonial expansion starting in the 1400s. Wine lasted a fairly long time and was easily transported. Sailors consumed it and it was a valuable trade item. One of the important wines traded from Portugal was madeira wine, from Madeira island. The madeira wine trade was mainly focused on the Atlantic trade; it went to Britain, the Caribbean, and Portuguese Brazil. The island of Madeira was strategically located between England, the North American colonies, and the Caribbean. Not only did madeira wine go to Europe and the Americas, but it also became an important trade item to India through the East India Trading Company and others in the eighteenth-century. Interestingly, as the ships sailed to tropical ports and temperatures in the hull where the barrels were stored rose to over 100 degrees Fahrenheit, madeira wine improved in quality. So oceanic trade in and of itself actually increased the marketability of this important alcoholic product. In addition to madeira wine, port, a fortified wine from the Doura valley in Portugal, became popular in England during the early eighteenth-century, making substantial income for Portugal. Much like for Spain, commercial alcohol became an important way for Portugal to expand its trade into many parts of the world.

The important shipping giant in the Atlantic World, however, was the Dutch. Not only did they ship their own goods, but also those of other Northern and Southern European countries as well. One of their most important trade items was alcohol. The Dutch became highly involved in the wine trade, not only shipping wine throughout Europe and to the colonies, but also influencing how wine was produced in France, particularly the Bordeaux region. They taught the French to burn sulphur in barrels before filling them with wine. This technique added to the stability of the wines as they were shipped. Dutch shippers also carried brandy from France to England and to other parts of Northern Europe. Brandy became an extremely valuable item of trade. Sailors drank it on ships because it was more easily transported than wine. And it became popular in ports of call as well as in many parts of France. Brandy became the best way to transform otherwise poor-quality wine into a profitable commodity. Moreover, the popularity of brandy increased alcohol consumption across Europe. Shipping brandy and wine bolstered the strong trade position of the Dutch in the colonial period.

France became involved in the alcohol trade as well. Its role in the trade influenced the development of new kinds of wine in France. For example, champagne became popular among European elites during the seventeenth-century, and demand for champagne increased its production. In addition, merchants introduced new kinds of wines by mixing existing wines in order to stabilize them during shipping. As varieties of wines became more recognizable it became more common to distinguish wine drinking between classes. For example, dark red wine was thought to be better for the lower classes, while white and lighter reds were better for elites. Thus trade in wine further defined alcohol consumption patterns, helping to differentiate between classes. The alcohol trade also helped to define the relationship between France and its colonies. France outlawed the importation of rum from the French West Indies as a way to protect the brandy and wine producers at home.

West Africa

As an important commodity alcohol not only helped to shape the trade in slaves from West Africa, but the influx of Western alcohols also transformed drinking habits in ways that would have far-reaching social consequences in the future. Moreover, alcohol made vast profits for those European countries that traded it. Europeans not only traded alcohol for slaves, but also for other important commodities, such as rubber, wax, palm oil, and ivory. These raw materials supplied the beginnings of industrialization in Europe.

Indigenous alcohol was used in Africa, likely since the beginnings of agriculture. Fermented from grains, honey, fruit, palm trees, and milk, alcohol use had been highly regulated by tribal leaders. As early as the fifteenth-century

Europeans began purchasing slaves from Western Africa, trading, among other things, grape wine and distilled spirits such as rum, gin, and brandy. It was distilled spirits, however, that elicited tremendous demand among the Western Africans.

One distilled spirit in particular, rum, became a central ingredient in the famous triangle Atlantic trade. Rum was shipped to the New England colonies in exchange for lumber and grain to be used on the sugar plantations in the Caribbean and Brazil. Caribbean and Brazilian distillers shipped rum to Western Africa to be given as gifts to African kings, and to be used as a secondary trade item for slaves, who then were shipped back to the Caribbean and Brazil. Alcohol became so important to the slave trade that by the late eighteenth-century Western Africa was purchasing almost three million liters of alcohol per year, and by the mid-nineteenth-century almost 24 million liters per year. In the overall Atlantic slave trade in its 300 year history, perhaps 5 to 10 percent of all slaves were purchased with European alcohol.

The Portuguese, especially, relied on alcohol in their trade for slaves in Angola. For example, in the seventeenth-century Portuguese wine was in such high demand by African slave traders that some merchants made up to 500 percent profit in this trade during the 1600s. Moreover, the Portuguese in Brazil began to produce a great deal of cheap distilled liquor from sugarcane, called cachaça, or gerebita, to trade for slaves. This cheap, slave-produced, sugarcane brandy was popular among the slaves in Brazil, and it was popular as a trade item in Africa for more slaves. As a result of the increased Brazilian production of cachaça in the late seventeenth through the early nineteenth-centuries, coastal Brazil gained tremendous power over the slave trade in Angola. Records indicate that 25 percent of the almost 1.2 million slaves sold out of Angola in the eighteenth-century were bought with Brazilian cachaça.

As a result of trading alcohol for slaves, drinking patterns in West Africa changed dramatically. Not only did elites begin to drink European alcohol, but the demand for alcohol also filtered down to the majority of the population, increasing their alcohol consumption and changing the village social dynamics. African leaders no longer controlled alcohol use in their villages. Young African merchants, having earned their own money, gained increased access to the European alcohols, usurping the time-honored power of village elders to control the right to use alcohol.

South Africa

Western Europe not only traded slaves from the coast of West Africa, but it also penetrated South Africa in the period between the sixteenth- and eighteenth-centuries. The Dutch in South Africa began by searching for spices in the sixteenth-century. When they found none, they believed the area to be of little use except to resupply their ships that were headed to Southeast Asia. European immigrants to South Africa realized the value of wine in fueling these trading ships. In the seventeenth-century when Cape Town was founded, transplanted grape vines from areas such as France were soon planted. Again, the grapes were to be made into wine solely to restock ships sailing to Southeast Asia. Due to just a few men, including Jan van Riebeeck and Simon van der Stel, wine growing became popular in South Africa. When French Huguenots immigrated to the area they brought their wine-making expertise and helped the growing industry in Cape Town. Even though the industry was growing, South Africa was not known for high-quality wine. The tremendous demand for wine on the trading and exploration ships, however, fueled the growth of the wine industry in South Africa, helping to shape the economy of that region.

North America

The story of alcohol in colonial North America was one of social, cultural, economic, and political influence. In North America colonists all along the east coast continually attempted to grow wine. They used the liquor themselves, believing that alcohol, especially beer and wine, was essential to their daily lives. Alcohol structured their days; they used beer for food, medicine, and as a medium for socializing. Alcohol not only supplied the lives of the colonists, but it also fueled trade with Native Americans. Demand was so high that Native Americans would trade virtually anything to gain access to it, earning European traders incredible profits. Moreover, as a result of the influx of the previously unknown alcohol, Native American cultural rituals changed, as they began to believe inebriation allowed them to communicate with the spirits.

Both the British and French colonial governments became involved with alcohol, too. Each of them heavily relied on alcohol taxes, yet at the same time, they also tried to control alcohol use, many times as a façade meant to actually control marginalized segments of society. The government focused on public drunkenness and began to highly regulate taverns, correctly believing taverns to be responsible for fomenting political rebellion, since taverns acted as the primary gathering places for men in villages, towns, and even cities. Finally, the French and British governments in Europe vied for the extremely profitable colonial alcohol market, exacerbating their already heated rivalry in the European political arena.

In New England most colonists produced their own alcohol for personal consumption. For example, householders produced their own ale, cider, and brandy. Moreover, because they believed beer to be so important for the health of the colonists, the Virginia colony asked Britain to send over brewers to the colony, and the colony of Massachusetts established its own brewery in 1629. The Puritans in Massachusetts, like the Virginians, believed that beer was essential for the good health of their people. The Dutch in New York and New Jersey also set up breweries as well as taverns, especially in New Amsterdam (New York City). Beer continued to be important in the North

American diet throughout the eighteenth-century and into the period of the war for independence. During the revolutionary period a "buy American" campaign emerged and the constant demand for beer resulted in it becoming one of the targeted commodities to be made exclusively in North America instead of being imported from England.

Beer was not the only preferred form of alcohol in the North American colonies. In the early seventeenth-century North American colonists were urged to produce their own wine. For example, in Jamestown, colonists were required to plant vines and to learn how to make wine. The area was not conducive to wine making, however. The New England colonists started out with the same idea. They believed that because there were so many wild grapes in the area that wine making would flourish. The wild grapes that grew in the New England colonies were not conducive to wine making, however, and the vines that were imported from Europe soon died of various diseases. Colonists in many other areas also tried to make wine and eventually ended up failing. Georgia, South Carolina, Virginia, New Jersey, Louisiana, and Pennsylvania all had failed wine-making attempts. Wine remained so important to the colonists that attempts continued to be made, even though they continued to fail.

Colonists not only produced alcohol for themselves, but they also traded it with Native Americans. As a result of Native American enthusiasm for alcohol the Europeans traded it to them in exchange for their land and other goods such as furs, and sometimes even sexual access to their wives. The Native American demand for alcohol also remained continuous because, unlike other consumer goods, alcohol always needed to be replenished. In fact, the biggest profits for the traders came from trading alcohol, sometimes as much as 400 percent. Not only did the British traders benefit from the trade in alcohol but the French also made extremely high profits from the trade. French trading policies in the North American colonies allowed French Caribbean sugar (desired to be made into alcohol) to be sold at a lower price than British produced sugar, earning profits for the French and fostering the continued rivalry with the British. Even the British North American colonists sold rum made from French colonial molasses to the Native Americans, causing even more competition between the British and French. As a result, those British who owned the sugar plantations in the British Caribbean lost money. The North American colonists continued the practice, however, and made enough money from this trade to buy manufactured goods from England.

Consumption of alcohol influenced the lives of North American colonists as much or more so than production and trade. Colonists consumed alcohol instead of water because the lack of potable water made water an unsafe option. They also used alcohol for medicinal purposes. They used it for fever, indigestion, and general aches and pains. In colonial North America alcohol was also central to nutrition and social functions. Alcohol was so important to the diets of the colonists that George Washington ordered that soldiers be given beer and cider as part of their food rations.

Not only did colonists imbibe, but also Native Americans began drinking after colonization. Native Americans had not been exposed to alcohol before the arrival of the colonists. A perhaps apocryphal story from 1609 tells of Hudson's expedition that came upon Native Americans fishing in the bay of New York. Meeting them on an island, an Englishman offered alcohol (after having drunk the first cup himself), but the chief would not drink it. Instead, a warrior came forward, drank the alcohol, and then passed out. After he woke up he declared it was the best experience he had ever had. The rest of the group then drank the alcohol and they all became drunk. As a result, the Delaware Indians called the place Manahachtanienk, or "the island where we all got drunk." The island was later named Manhattan.

Some Native Americans had used hallucinogenic drugs before the arrival of the Europeans, so they believed that alcohol, too, contained magical powers and the ability to help them communicate with the spirits. Therefore, the goal of consuming alcohol was to become extremely inebriated, and enter into an altered state able to commune with the gods. An account of the time by an English traveler observed that the Native Americans drank in enough quantity to get very drunk. If there was not enough alcohol for everyone in the group to become entirely intoxicated, then some would abstain completely, allowing just a few of the members of the group to experience total inebriation. Some authors have argued, however, that the comportment of Native Americans when drinking came from mimicking the drinking behavior of the Europeans. Whatever the case, alcohol embedded itself into indigenous culture.

Regulation of alcohol also influenced the development of the colonies. Both the British and French colonial governments regulated the alcohol trade. Regulation sometimes reflected the ambivalence of the British and French authorities, however. For example, the British authorities disapproved of the alcohol trade with the Native Americans, while at the same time collecting significant tax revenues from it. Taxes on alcohol helped support colonial governments, especially the growth of infrastructure. The French colonial government approved of the trade with Native Americans in some contexts, but the French clerical authorities disapproved, so much so, that in order to receive absolution for trading alcohol with the Indians one needed to go to a regional bishop or all the way to the Pope. Ambivalence regarding the alcohol trade did not stop Britain and France from fighting over the profits, however.

In 1733, in yet another move in the competition between the British and the French, the British Parliament passed the Molasses Act, which added exorbitant duties on foreign molasses imported into the British North American colonies from the French colonies. The English colonists did not obey this law and continued to purchase cheaper molasses and rum from the French West Indies. In 1764, then, Parliament passed the Sugar Act, which was designed to replace the Molasses Act. The tax on the British colonists for sugar and molasses was lowered, but was more strictly enforced. In addition, other items, including wine (except French wine), were taxed. Parliament justified this act by stating in the act that it needed to increase revenue to the crown in return for protecting the colonies. As a consequence of this stricter law, rum production in the British North American colonies decreased. This resulted in a decline in available currency in the North American colonies, and the decreased ability to buy manufactured goods from England, which, ironically, hurt industries in England where the law was passed. Implicit in the act was a strong anti-French sentiment. The intensity of the fight to regulate the importation of sugar and molasses destined for alcohol production reveals the significance of alcohol as a pawn in the competition between European states to control the colonies in the New World.

Government regulations also covered taverns. Taverns that sold beer were also regulated by the 1630s. The price of beer was fixed and tavern keepers had to have a license. Regulations on producing beer also emerged. For example, it was illegal to brew beer at home; beer had to be bought at taverns. By the eighteenth-century taverns became even more regulated because taverns began to be seen as possible centers of working-class rebellion.

The British government not only regulated the trade in alcohol but also regulated its consumption. Early on alcohol use did not pose any great problem, even though each community had those who were labeled as drunkards. Laws concerning alcohol in the colonies eventually responded to abuses by colonists and Native Americans, however. Parliament gave local North American courts the right to levy fines for public drunkenness. The authorities believed that excessive alcohol consumption led to other crimes such as physical violence, adultery, and even murder. Not only the government, but also the church regulated consumption. The strong social structure of Puritanism worked to control excessive drinking during the first 50 years of the colony in New England. Wine, seemingly, was one of the problematic substances – second only to whiskey and rum. Wine historian Rod Phillips points out:

> In 1645 a definition of excessive drinking was established; half a pint of wine per person on any occasion. ... [Moreover,] [i]n 1677, for example, only seven of the twenty-seven men and women licensed to sell alcohol [in Massachusetts] were permitted to sell wine ... Laws were also passed to forbid drinking to anyone's health, providing drink as part of wages, and furnishing rations of drink above and beyond wages.

Clearly abuse of alcohol had become something of a problem in the British North American colonies. In addition to wine, however, the increase in the consumption of spirits, especially rum and whiskey, also led to high rates of drunkenness. As a result, stricter regulation was aimed at spirits much more so than ale or beer. Governmental strategies to control the intake of alcohol among the colonists and Native Americans included outlawing its production in many areas. Catholic and Protestant missionaries, as well as the colonists themselves, wanted to control drinking.

Latin America

Alcohol production, trade, consumption, and regulation influenced the development of colonial Latin America in several ways. Latin American-produced spirits drove a good portion of the Atlantic trading system and became the primary trade good for many islands in the Caribbean. Within Latin America the introduction of distilled alcohol forever altered indigenous drinking patterns, social behavior, and culture. The Spaniards introduced distillation into Mexico, stimulating an already growing demand for alcohol among the Native Mexicans. As a result, indigenous consumption patterns radically changed. Whereas alcohol in pre-conquest Mexico had only been available to the general population during festivals and rituals, it was now available all the time; and with the introduction of the Spanish cultural habit of drinking daily, many indigenous over-consumed. The Aztec social mores that had regulated drinking before the conquest no longer existed, so not only did indigenous Mexicans drink more, but more indigenous drank.

Spirits were popular, but native Mexicans primarily drank fermented pluque. As the indigenous population rebounded from the demographic devastation of the conquest, pulque demand skyrocketed. Men especially drank high quantities of pulque, enough for society to equate indigenous masculine identity with alcohol consumption. Moreover, indigenous use of alcohol seemed to provide the most effective way for Native Mexicans to passively resist labor exploitation by the Spaniards. Because of such high demand, the pulque trade provided an opportunity for many to make a great deal of money. The fact that women dominated the small-scale trade while men controlled the large-scale trade began to solidify not only gender identity, but also gender hierarchies within the villages.

Alcohol consumption pattern also signified cultural identity. While native Mexicans drank pulque, Spaniards, who desperately attempted to grow grape vines all over Latin America, demanded wine. Moreover, the Spaniards valued the ability to "hold one's liquor," while many indigenous drank to unconsciousness. In the view of the Spanish, their taste in wine, as well as their supposedly restrained consumption habits, not only set them apart from indigenous culture, but also demonstrated their cultural superiority. Many indigenous also recognized the power of alcohol to distinguish culture. Native Mexicans clandestinely continued to use alcohol in pre-colonial religious rituals, providing a tangible way to maintain their pre-conquest religion and culture. At the same time, the custom of using alcohol in religious rituals and on religious holidays united Catholicism with Mexican religions, allowing Indians to more easily synchronize their religious beliefs with Catholicism.

The colonial governments in Latin America, however, wrestled with the complex role of alcohol in society. Spaniards attempted to limit indigenous consumption, ostensibly to maintain social order, yet in effect to control just another aspect of the lives of the colonized. At the same time that the colonial governments espoused the benefits of moderation with one hand, however, with the other hand they enthusiastically collected substantial alcohol taxes, which they relied upon to fund their colonial project. In essence, alcohol shaped colonial society.

Distilled alcohol became an essential trade item for Latin America in the Atlantic trading system, especially for the Caribbean. Perhaps the most important distilled liquor introduced in the New World was rum. Rum was invented in the sixteenth-century in the Latin American island colonies and was most commonly distilled from sugarcane juice and the scum, or skimmed waste, from sugar production. Barbados by the late 1600s, for example, produced approximately one million gallons of rum, and Martinique produced almost half that amount. The British Caribbean island of Jamaica became the largest producer of rum in the eighteenth-century, and in the 1770s was exporting more than two million gallons per year.

Distilled liquors changed the nature of alcohol consumption in the new world. Its high alcohol content, 40 percent or more in some cases, dwarfed the 2 to 12 percent in the existing fermented beverages, and consumers tended to become much more inebriated than they did on ale, beer, or wine, leading to a tremendous rise in alcohol-related problems such as public drunkenness and violence. Distillers in the Caribbean also made rum for the European colonists who lived on the islands because many kinds of alcohol were too expensive to import from Europe, and the colonists demanded a steady supply of some kind of alcohol.

When Europeans arrived in mainland Latin America they found the indigenous already producing alcohol. In Mesoamerica several kinds of alcohol existed and were used before colonization. All of these were directly fermented from fruit or cacti. One of the most popular drinks in pre-colonial central Mexico was pulque, discussed in the previous chapter. The Spanish introduced distillation technology to Mesoamerica in the sixteenth-century distilling pulque into a spirit called mezcal. The Spanish experimented with several of the at least 200 species of agave in Mexico until they found the best ones to make mezcal.

Mexicans still produced impressive amounts of pulque, however. Elite Mexico City families owned pulque ranches outside of Mexico City and these ranches produced much of the pulque sold in the city. There were also small towns within a 15-mile radius of Mexico City that specialized in making pulque, and for many of these towns pulque was their main source of income. There were peasants who individually became rich off of the pulque trade. Especially by the eighteenth-century there were those who had built up large pulque productions in many villages. This exacerbated social stratification within indigenous society. By the second half of the eighteenth-century Jesuits had founded very profitable pulque haciendas, and after the Bourbon Reforms, elites in New Spain controlled the pulque trade, garnering tremendous profits.

Women dominated the small time trade in pulque. Most of the time it was women who took the pulque from the pulque villages to Mexico City to sell. And in the villages it was women who sold pulque from the doorways of their homes, because of the lack of permanent pulquerías in small villages. The small taverns that did exist were owned by widows. Consequently, women's role as small-time purveyors of pulque not only provided for their economic independence, but also acted as a key component of their female gender identity.

While Native Mexicans focused on the production of pulque, many Spaniards focused on wine. Spaniards not only shipped wine from Spain and Portugal to the New World, but they also began to cultivate wine there. By the 1550s there were vineyards in Mexico, the Andean region, as well as Chile and Argentina. The vines came from Europe because of the lack of suitable vines in the new world. In fact, Cortes, the leader of the conquistadores in Mexico, ordered his encomenderos (those who were given large tracts of land and the labor of the indigenous on that land) to plant grape vines. One thousand grape vines were supposed to be planted for every 100 indigenous workers under the command of an encomendero. Workers grafted European grape vines onto native grape vines in order to create the best possible combination.

Central Mexican viticulture did not work well, however, because of the climate, but Northern Mexico began to be known as a wine-growing region. The missions in California, in particular, began to grow grapes and make wine. So by the eighteenth-century California missions were making thousands of gallons of wine and brandy, although wine making was not a full-scale industry in California until much later. South American climates were also suited to produce wine and these wines circulated throughout Latin America. It was deemed necessary to start viticulture and viniculture in Latin America because shipping wine from Spain was so expensive and there was a high Spanish demand in the colonies. The growing worldwide significance of wine as a status symbol further demonstrated to the Spanish that their taste for wine not only widened the cultural gap between them and the indigenous, but also solidified their racial superiority in Latin America.

Within the Spanish colonies, however, issues over wine production existed. The wine producers in Spain were not happy with wine production in the New World because it competed with the sale of their wine. The Spanish wine growers counted on the colonial markets for substantial profits. The problem became great enough that Philip II of Spain restricted the planting of vine-yards in the New World in 1595. Many colonial wine makers ignored these restrictions, however. Another problem with the growing wine industry, according to Spanish authorities in Mexico, concerned unscrupulous wine sellers who sold wine to unsuspecting Indian villagers in order to get them drunk and cheat them out of their land. The Spaniards could buy indigenous land for much lower than the actual value with alcohol. While wine was not the common alcoholic drink of the indigenous, wine sellers were still successful in their attempts to dupe intoxicated Indians into selling their land. Moreover, because wine had not been a part of the ritual structure of indigenous life before the conquest, the abuse of it was much more common and it caused more social unrest in the villages, especially in the sixteenth- and early seventeenth-centuries when this practice occurred. Consequently, wine production and sale, then, furthered both the Spanish exploitation of the Indians as well as social unrest within indigenous communities.

In Portuguese Brazil, colonization and trade brought new kinds of alcohol to that colony. The Portuguese colonists began planting vineyards as soon as they colonized Brazil in the 1530s. This failed, however, because the climate was not conducive to wine grape growing. In addition, the Portuguese merchants in Portugal did not want the competition for their products. As a result, sugarcane-based alcohol began to be produced. Two very popular types of alcohol made from sugarcane were cachaça and aguardiente. Cachaça was made by fermenting the leftover juices from sugar production. It was then boiled, which increased the alcohol content. These sugarcane-based alcohols became very popular with the slaves in Brazil.

Colonization not only transformed alcohol production, but also consumption. The Spaniards introduced new consumption patterns to the Aztecs because Spanish and Aztec consumption patterns differed. Spaniards not only drank wine on religious holidays, but they also drank wine daily with meals. They did not have the habit of complete drunkenness, however. In fact, the Spanish believed that to call someone a drunkard was considered the worst possible insult one could level against another person. In contrast to the Spaniards, the indigenous Mexicans before the conquest drank pulque mainly for ritual purposes. As a result of the Spanish example, though, alcohol consumption by the indigenous lower classes increased considerably after the conquest. Some sources argue that the Native Americans began to drink daily like the Spaniards, but also continued their former style of drinking, which was drinking until they passed out. The combination had disastrous effects.

In addition, there was an increase in the number of people who drank because the social mores of the Aztecs that prevented many people from drinking had broken down. The numerous Catholic religious holidays and the commercialization of pulque brought on increased abuse as well. Other indications of increased drinking included the creation of taverns and inns in the countryside along travel routes that served pulque and wine, as well as the increased household production of pulque for family use.

People especially drank pulque during the dry season, from October to May, because pulque took the place of water and because the two major Catholic holidays, Christmas and Easter, took place during this period. Many people drank pulque during the day with meals and in the fields while they worked. In addition, the weekly market common in many small towns brought in people from the countryside who used the occasion to drink excessively. The indigenous also drank to excess on Sundays because they thought of Sunday as a religious holiday and because they had the day off from work. People also drank pulque during communal work days, either working in a neighbor's fields or working for the community. Moreover, pulque continued to be used as medicine among the indigenous. Men drank more pulque than women did, which was commonly accepted by the community as a masculine trait. Problems arose, however, when men drank so much that they could not carry out their daily work duties.

Violence also occurred as a result of drinking too much. In some areas drinking preceded many homicides, and in other places it led to fights among villagers. Where violence and drinking mixed to the greatest degree was in and around taverns. These taverns, or pulquerías, were numerous in Mexico City, and offered music, dancing, spicy food, gambling, and prostitution. Social mores seemed to be left at the door of these establishments. Those living in Mexico City drank more often and in larger quantities than did those in the countryside. William Taylor, in *Drinking, Homicide, and Rebellion* notes that in 1783 "the consumption of pulque reached 187 gallons for every adult resident of the city – plus perhaps three gallons of distilled alcohol." Thus new alcohol consumption patterns that included abuse of alcohol exacerbated the social breakdown of the indigenous societies after the conquest. Indigenous drinking became a problem for the Spaniards who sought to control the behavior of the native Mexicans. Spaniards believed that drinking to intoxication led to a breakdown of society because "drunken Indians" were no longer able to be controlled. Moreover, the Spanish, who considered it manly to be able to control one's behavior while drinking, identified drunkenness as a social malady; in a sadly ironic twist, the very drinking patterns introduced by the Spaniards themselves furthered their intense racism against Native Mexicans. Some scholars have argued, however, that indigenous alcohol abuse could be construed as passive resistance against the onerous labor expectations of the Spaniards, who used pulque to entice laborers to build infrastructure, to produce agriculture, and to extract silver.

Even though substantial changes occurred in drinking patterns after the conquest, some continuities remained. Many indigenous village elites continued to practice ceremonies honoring local gods. William Taylor notes the holdovers from pre-conquest drinking patterns. "Animal sacrifices accompanied by community drinking were thought to protect the community from new diseases brought by the Spaniards." So the native Mexicans used pulque in pre-conquest ritual ways, but for new reasons brought on by colonialism. Indigenous leaders also encouraged ritual drinking by commoners as a way to turn them away from Catholic missionary efforts. In addition, pulque continued to be used at marriage ceremonies, at births and deaths, and at harvest ceremonies. However, alcohol also facilitated some syncretism between pre-conquest religions and Catholicism. For example, one group of elite Indians honored the stars by drinking pulque, but on Sunday nights, a Catholic holy day. So in some ways ritual pulque use helped maintain traditional culture in the face of colonialism, but in other ways consumption patterns furthered cultural miscegenation between Indians and Spaniards.

In Latin America the colonial governments had to control much larger centers of population than did the North American colonial governments, and regulating alcohol consumption was central to social control. The colonial Latin American government believed that the indigenous were prone to drunkenness and violent behavior and thus needed special rules regarding liquor. Tensions over regulations arose within the colonial government and between the colonial government and the merchants, however. On the one hand the colonial government relied on high consumption levels for the substantial taxes brought in by alcohol, which also worked in favor of the merchants who just wanted to sell their product. On the other hand the government sought to control Native Mexican behavior through limiting their access to alcohol.

The Spanish king had to repeatedly impose regulations because indigenous alcohol abuse, resulting from the sale of liquor by colonial merchants as well as the church, remained such a problem. In 1524 Phillip II outlawed the sale of any kind of alcohol to indigenous Mexicans. By 1572 the crown tried to control the sale of Spanish wine to Indians by requiring licenses and then by banning the sale of wine to Indians altogether in 1594, 1637, and 1640. The sale of Spanish wine to indigenous villagers continued, however, because of the tremendous profits that could be made. Not only did regular Spanish merchants take part in this trade, but Catholic bishops worked their way into the profitable trade as well. Indigenous village leaders did not sit by passively and allow this influx of wine to ruin their villages' social order, however. Many villages demanded that the viceroy enforce the laws against selling wine to indigenous Mexicans.

William Taylor explains several laws that were instituted to control the pulque trade. In 1579, 1585, and 1586 it became illegal to sell pulque, wine, and maguey syrup except in a few regulated areas in Mexico City. In 1608 the viceroy went so far as to order that only one "respectable old woman" per every 100 Indians could gain a license to sell pulque. Because there was such a large black market in the pulque trade, however, in 1635 and 1639 it became illegal to bring pulque into the city, except during the day. By 1692, however, pulque production was outlawed again because of a Mexico City riot, blamed on "drunken Indians." At the same time, however, the colonial government benefitted from not enforcing the bans on the sale of pulque because of the staggering tax revenues it brought in, which were needed for the growth of infrastructure. The government issued permits to make wine and beer as a strategy to raise tax revenue. The number of petitions for licenses to sell pulque in Mexico City and other populated areas in the sixteenth- and seventeenth-centuries were very high. Once again, however, in the eighteenth-century Spanish colonial officials outlawed pulque because they believed it led to disturbances, although that law lasted only five years. Thus the colonial government remained ambivalent about the sale of alcohol to indigenous Mexicans.

The Spanish monarchy also regulated rum production in its Caribbean colonies. In 1693, all rum making was outlawed in the Spanish colonies. The Spanish officials believed that rum competed too heavily with the Spanish alcohols imported into the colonies. Moreover, these colonial officials were nervous about what they believed to be the overindulgence in rum by African slaves as well as by the indigenous population. They feared that drunkenness would lead to disorder, and could eventually lead to a slave insurrection.

This law was routinely ignored, however, as immediate profits outweighed concerns over potential problems.

In the Andean region the colonial government also regulated alcohol consumption. Chicha, or corn beer, was a staple drink in the Andes. Much like pulque, it had been used for ceremonial purposes throughout the period of Inca rule and before. After colonization, however, the Spanish believed that many problems arose because of excessive chicha use by indigenous South Americans. For example, in 1556, judge Gregorio Gonzales de Cuenca ordered that drinking be stopped. He said:

> Because ... chiefs and leaders used to have 'taverns' and places where all who came to them were given chicha to drink, and it is the cause of the drunkenness of the people, and it occupies many men and women in making the chicha, and it is a thing of bad example, and the said chiefs and leaders spend excessively on it; it is ordered that from now on they (the chiefs) not have such 'taverns' nor public or secret places for drinking ...
>
> (as quoted in Gastineau *et al. Fermented Food Beverages in Nutrition*)

So even though the Spaniards throughout Latin America believed that alcohol caused problems with Native Latin Americans, they used alcohol to further the colonial project as well as to solidify social stratification between the Spaniards and the indigenous. Alcohol played a complex role in Latin American society throughout the colonial period.

Conclusion

In many ways the production, trade, consumption, and regulation of alcohol fostered European success in world trade, helped to solidify the new colonial identities of both the colonists and the indigenous, and structured the ways in which the colonial powers subjugated native North and South Americans. First, both the colonists in North America as well as the indigenous in Latin America fermented their own alcohol because alcohol sustained their nutritional, social, and cultural lives. Second, North American, South African, and Latin American colonists all made repeated attempts at growing grapes for wine because wine not only structured their daily lives, but also seemed to be an essential part of their very identities as Europeans in a foreign land. Third, rum and other liquors fueled the triangle trade in the fifteenth through the nineteenth-centuries, allowing many European states to buy a significant number of slaves because of the high demand for alcohol from African slave traders. Fourth, the colonists in North America and Latin America forcefully sold alcohol to the indigenous, which in North America led to unscrupulous land deals, and in Latin America, social breakdown.

Fifth, alcohol was key in the colonial labor exploitation of both Africans and indigenous Latin Americans. Sixth, Spain, Portugal, the Netherlands, and

France all competed for markets in the lucrative wine trade, which intensified the struggle for power among these European states. Seventh, colonial alcohol producers competed against European alcohol producers for alcohol markets, thus exacerbating the hierarchy that privileged the European states over their colonies.

Consumption of alcohol in the early-modern period disrupted native social structures, created new colonial identities, and created new cultural practices in several ways. First, the introduction of alcohol changed the consumption habits of Native North Americans, West Africans, and Native Latin Americans. In the case of the North Americans they had not previously been introduced to alcohol; in the case of West Africans and Native Latin Americans alcohol consumption had been strictly regulated before contact by indigenous leaders. Thus the tremendous upsurge in drinking caused at best social disorder and at worst social disintegration in all three areas. Third, both in Africa and Latin America the power of indigenous leaders over alcohol consumption diminished, leading to a collapse of the traditional social hierarchy. Fourth, a clash of alcohol cultures led to virtual daily overindulgence by many native North and South Americans. Prior to colonization, Native Latin Americans drank only on ritual occasions, consuming enough alcohol to become completely inebriated and eventually black out. Native North Americans, after the Europeans introduced alcohol to them, also drank to reach complete drunkenness. Yet European alcohol habits called for social drinking on a daily basis. The combination of the two styles led to catastrophic social problems. Fifth, both in North America and in Latin America excessive consumption of alcohol led to violence, which again disrupted social harmony in the population.

Sixth, alcohol use for religious purposes differed between the colonists and the indigenous in both North America and South America. In North America, Protestantism espoused moderation, while Native Americans believed in the necessity of altered states to communicate with the spirits, causing a serious cultural clash of religious practices. In Latin America, however, while the frequency of Catholic holy days led the indigenous to celebrate more often than had been their custom, the similar custom of practicing religion with alcohol allowed the indigenous to more easily accept Catholicism.

Alcohol regulations affected Europe, Africa, and the New World colonies in numerous ways. First, the complex role of alcohol in the colonies led to contradictory policies regarding drinking. On the one hand the colonial governments in North America and Latin America both wanted to regulate the drinking of the indigenous because they wanted to control their behavior. On the other hand, the alcohol business was so lucrative that both governments came to depend upon the taxes garnered from the trade. Second, alcohol regulations were used as a tool in the competition between the British and the French for power both in the colonies and in Europe. Third, even within the Catholic Church in the colonies contradictory approaches to alcohol existed. While Catholics in North America wanted to curb alcohol excesses, the

Catholic Church in Latin America was deeply involved in the alcohol trade, focusing on profits rather than regulation. Fourth, high levels of abuse that seriously disrupted the social order, as well as repeated non-compliance, led to governmental regulations that had to be repeatedly legislated in Mexico, Brazil, North America, and South America.

World trade and colonialism, the two major trends in the early modern period, were significantly influenced by the production, trade, consumption, and regulation of alcohol. The centrality of alcohol in the lives of people across cultures and continents necessitated its daily production by the indigenous as well as the colonists in Africa, North America, and South America. Trade of alcohol provided national as well as individual riches leading to competition among countries and to domestic competition across classes and racial divides. Alcohol also provided Europeans with an effective tool to exploit native West Africans, and North and South Americans, which helped lead to high levels of alcohol consumption by the indigenous in all three areas, causing a breakdown of their social order. Finally, contradictions between governmental regulation and taxation revealed that rather than being immutable, alcohol was a tool on the one hand for social control when necessary, and on the other hand for economic gain when necessary. In all its expressions, however, alcohol played a key role in early modern world trade as well as European colonization.

Further reading

Bennett, L. A. and G. M. Ames. 1985. *The American Experience with Alcohol: Contrasting Cultural Perspectives.* New York: Plenum Press.

Curto, J. 1996. *Alcohol and Slaves: The Luso-Brazilian Alcohol Commerce at Mpinda, Luanda, and Benguela during the Atlantic Slave trade c. 1480–1830 and its Impact on the Societies of West Central Africa.* Phd Dissertation. University of California Los Angeles.

——2006. *Enslaving Spirits: The Portuguese-Brazilian Alcohol Trade at Luanda and its Hinterland, c. 1550–1830.* Boston, MA: Brill.

Gastineau, C. F., W. J. Darby, and T. B. Turner. 1979. *Fermented Food Beverages in Nutrition.* New York: Academic Press.

Hyams, E. 1965. *A Social History of the Wine Vine: Dionysus.* New York: The Macmillian Company.

Jankowiak, W. and D. Bradburd. (eds.) 2003. *Drugs, Labor, and Colonial Expansion.* Tuscon: University of Arizona Press.

Kicza, J. E. 1980. "The Pulque Trade of Late Colonial Mexico City." *The Americas.* 37 (2): 193–221.

——1991. "Drinking, popular protest, and governmental response in seventeenth- and eighteenth-century Latin America." *Contemporary Drug Problems.* 18 (2): 219–36.

MacAndrew, Cr. and R. B. Edgerton. 1969. *Drunken Comportment: A Social Explanation.* Chicago: Aldine Publishing Company.

Scardaville, M. C. 1980. "Alcohol Abuse and Tavern Reform in Late Colonial Mexico City." *The Hispanic American Historial Review.* 60 (4): 643–71.

Taylor, W. B. 1979. *Drinking, Homicide, and Rebellion in Colonial Mexican Villages.* Stanford, CA: Stanford University Press.

5   Alcohol, industrialization, and temperance in the nineteenth- and early twentieth-centuries

Industrialization transformed the world in the eighteenth-, nineteenth-, and early twentieth-centuries. The West led the world in industrialization, which brought with it new forms of labor organization, increased urbanization, and the separation of work from home and leisure from work. All of these changes helped to define the lives of the emerging working and middle classes in particular. Industrialization also transformed the alcohol industry by making it possible to mass produce alcohol. As a result, new forms of production, trade, consumption, and regulation of alcohol influenced the ways that gender, class, ethnicity, politics, and indeed industrialization developed during the eighteenth- and nineteenth-centuries. Most notably, within the arena of alcohol regulation, a powerful and widespread movement, called temperance, developed as a result of the change in consumption patterns. Temperance was one of the most important international social movements of the nineteenth-century, especially in Protestant countries in the West.

Temperance movements in the industrializing West differed based on the religious and ethnic makeup of the countries. Great Britain and the United States were both Protestant countries, yet the large African American population in the United States influenced the development of temperance in that country. Ireland differed from both Britain and the United States because it had a Catholic majority, however, it also was controlled by a Protestant minority that championed temperance. Finally, France was a predominantly Catholic country and one of the world's principal wine-growing areas. It did not have widespread temperance. The non-Western industrializing areas of Japan and Russia did not experience the strong temperance movements characteristic of the Protestant West either.

Great Britain

Alcohol in Britain not only shaped class and gender identities, but also produced a widespread social movement. Mass produced alcohol production pushed out craftsmen and proletarianized the industry. Alcohol establishments, by being essentially segregated by class, also helped to create distinctive class cultures in Britain. Moreover, alcohol venues, namely pubs, acted as the primary social centers for working men, becoming part of a man's masculine identity in the new industrial age. Alcohol consumption also characterized class identity. Cheap gin became identified with the working class. Authorities aggressively regulated the spirit, and temperance movements rallied against it, attempting to control the social lives of the working class in order to insure industry an adequate supply of productive workers, and thus further the development of industry and the concentration of wealth with the owners of capital. Yet at the same time, from the working-class perspective alcohol helped them cope with their difficult lives and ameliorated the social upheavals and social restructuring necessitated by industrialization.

Industrialization transformed the production and trade of alcohol in Great Britain in the eighteenth- and nineteenth-centuries. Large, mechanized brewing houses began to be established, overtaking the cottage industry brewers and changing the beer trade. Large brewing families such as Guinness, Barclay, and Bass emerged during this period and became known as the "Princes of Trade." These large brewers began to sell their beer through a system called tied houses, which they also owned, making them "tied" to the individual brewer, so each house sold only one brand. Brewers expanded the tied system by buying up individually owned taverns or pubs across the country, thus acquiring more markets for their beer. The mechanization of the industry and the tying in of beer pubs, both of which displaced small brewers and began to standardize beer, did not diminish the popularity of pubs in that country, however.

More than simply outlets for beer, pubs developed into social centers for urban working-class men as well as centers for gaming and sports clubs. Cricket teams, football teams, domino players, and other game players met in pubs to talk about the game they had just finished, or to play games with their fellow drinkers. This kind of camaraderie brought men together, reinforcing stereotypically masculine gender roles. If women frequented these establishments they risked being stigmatized as prostitutes. In a few cases, however, pubs had a separate room with a separate entrance where women could drink without being seen by men. Nevertheless, the policies in drinking establishments helped to shape both male and female gender ideologies in the nineteenth-century.

Even though beer remained popular, Britain began to produce large quantities of gin. Gin could be distilled cheaper than beer could be brewed, and thus many brewers turned to distilling. For example, it took from between £2,000 and £10,000 to build a brewery, whereas it took only £500 to £5,000 to build a distillery. Over the eighteenth-century 25 percent of the pubs became gin shops in London. By the nineteenth-century even more alcohol sales focused on gin. "Dram" shops, shops that sold small glasses of spirits called drams, became more numerous as cheap gin rose in popularity with the working class. Many establishments, however, did not obtain licenses to sell spirits, and those that continued to trade in beer alone outnumbered those with spirits licenses. In many cities beerhouses were more popular with working-class men because their beer was cheap, and more importantly, they provided credit.

In addition to providing credit, pubs tried other strategies to maximize the amount of alcohol sold. They changed the layout. Pubs took out all seating, thus encouraging working-class men to crowd up to the bar and quickly order more to drink. These new establishments served no food, had sawdust floors, and only about 10 percent had bathrooms. These changes led to a decline in the respectability of pubs and caused the middle-class to look down upon the establishments and the working-class patrons who frequented them. What is more, virtually all establishments across Britain perpetuated class distinctions. Those of the working class populated the pubs, beerhouses, and dram shops, while those of the middle-class patronized what were called saloon bars, and those of the upper-class frequented private club houses. The separation of drinking establishments by class helped to solidify cultural and social identity among the classes in industrializing Britain.

Alcohol not only influenced identity, but it also shaped the practice of medicine. During the late nineteenth-century in Britain debates abounded regarding the medicinal use of alcohol. Even though the temperance movement was strong, using wine as medicine remained common. For example, a Dr. Francis Anstie wrote a book called *On the Uses of Wine in Health and Disease* in 1877. In this book he explained how wine should be used by those who were healthy and also how wine should be used by those with acute or chronic illnesses. He went on to note that for a healthy young woman a half a bottle a day of light wine was good, or if a young adult was quite active, then a bottle of wine a day was fine. For high fevers he prescribed diluted alcohol, and for typhoid fever he prescribed old sherry. Later books, written around the turn of the century, also lauded the benefits of wine on one's health. For example, these books argued that wine could be used for anemia, gout, and stomach problems.

Society viewed the consumption of spirits, however, in an entirely different light than that of wine. As the working class increasingly consumed more gin in the eighteenth-century the government reacted with stricter regulations. The government deemed gin such a problem that it raised taxes on it in order to slow down its consumption. The government imposed a tax of 20 shillings on every gallon in 1736. In addition, to open a gin shop one had to pay £50. The working class had such an obsession with gin that as a result of gin taxes riots broke out in London. Moreover, people found a way around the new laws. For example, according to John Watney in *Beer is Best: A History of Beer*, clever entrepreneurs set up chemist shops that sold "Cholick Water" that was actually gin. In addition, taverns began coloring the gin and selling it as wine. Another tactic gave gin new names, such as "Ladies' Delight." So despite attempts by the government to curb it, the consumption of gin continued to climb. Abuse of gin became such a problem among the working class in Britain that the government stopped requiring licenses for beer pubs in 1830 as an incentive to create more and cheaper places to drink beer instead of gin. This "Beer Act of 1830" did little to slow gin consumption, however.

Abuse of gin by the working class not only drew the attention of the government, but also of temperance movements. Temperance movements in Britain lauded the "benefits" of beer and condemned the "detriments" of gin as a way to decrease gin consumption. Many temperance advocates wrote poems that extolled the virtues of beer. For example, "Beer! Happy produce of our isle, Can sinewy strength impart, And, wearied with fatigue and toil, Can cheer each manly heart." Conversely, the poems written about gin told another story. "Gin! Cursed fiend with fury fraught, Makes human race a prey, It enters by a deadly draught, And steals our life away." (As quoted in John Watney *Beer is Best: A History of Beer.*) So according to both the government and temperance groups, beer actually helped society whereas gin caused severe problems.

Temperance movements used many tactics to slow down the consumption of gin and other alcohols in the nineteenth-century. Many segments of society joined in these efforts: men and women from both the middle and working classes as well as industrialists participated. Women in the Salvation Army for example formed the Drunkards Rescue Society in 1874 to help individuals with alcohol problems. In another strategy, one temperance group imported a program from Sweden. Called the Gothenburg system, it advocated hiring salaried managers to run pubs instead of owners. It was thought that the managers, seeing no profit incentive in pushing excessive drinking, would better manage consumption. In another approach, reformers advocated adding food back into pubs as well as other forms of entertainment in order to slow down drinking, which, when implemented, did result in lower consumption rates.

In the late nineteenth-century temperance tactics began to change. Instead of focusing on modifying personal behavior and upgrading alcohol venues temperance advocates began to promote wide-reaching legislation. As a result, more and more legislation against alcohol appeared. For example, the Intoxicating Liquor Act, or the Child Messenger Act, outlawed the sale of liquor to children under 14. In addition, the police could now arrest adults who were drunk in public places. In 1914 and 1915 the Defence of the Realm Act was passed, which gave the government the right to regulate the hours of pubs, to inspect breweries and pubs, to buy breweries, and to forbid the sale of certain kinds of alcohol such as absinthe. Finally by 1923 a new law forbade the sale of liquor to anyone under 18 unless that person was over 16 and wanted beer or cider with a meal. So, much of Britain's experience with alcohol in the eighteenth-, nineteenth-, and early twentieth-centuries focused on its regulation, as alcohol control became emblematic of a progressive, well-ordered society, one that controlled the growing working-class.

Ireland

Alcohol consumption in the largely Catholic country of Ireland shaped class, gender, and religious identities, while regulation provided the government with a socially sanctioned tool to control the working class. Alcohol consumption in Ireland skyrocketed in the eighteenth-century. The working class, in an attempt to cope with their lives in Irish urban slums, drank prodigious amounts of alcohol. Moreover, much like in other areas in the West, pubs became male working-class bastions, adding to the new definitions of both masculinity and class, and furthering the separation between work and leisure. Drinking alcohol became something one did outside of work, rather than at points during the workday as had been the case before industrialization. Not only did men drink alcohol away from work, but the increase in the number of urban pubs meant that most alcohol consumption took place in public drinking establishments. The urban working-class led the way in making public drinking a predominant form of leisure.

Whiskey consumption by the working class rose, leading to a flood of anti-whiskey propaganda across society. Both the government and temperance movements attempted to regulate it, and by proxy increase working-class industrial productivity and influence the cultural construction of that class. Alcohol abuse by the urban working class brought on the incumbent problems of violence, absenteeism, and health troubles. Moreover, the Protestant elite characterized Catholics as drunkards, claiming degeneracy of that entire subculture as a result of their alcohol consumption. So Catholics, too, championed temperance as a way to become socially acceptable to the British.

Consumption of alcohol in Ireland, particularly whiskey, jumped in the modern period. For example, in the eighteenth-century the population of Ireland grew by 50 percent, while the consumption of spirits, especially whiskey, grew by almost 750 percent. Whiskey consumption continued to increase in the nineteenth-century with industrialization of the whiskey industry. The mass produced whiskey became more accessible to the working class because it was so cheap. In contrast to the urban working-class, the rural poor still did not have enough disposable income to drink heavily, and the gentry drank wine and not whiskey. These disparate alcohol consumption patterns, then, furthered the cultural gap between the working-class, the gentry, and the rural poor.

Regulation of alcohol in Ireland responded primarily to the problems of whiskey abuse by the urban working-class. The government tried various regulations to slow down its production, including lowering taxes on beer so drinkers would turn to it and away from whiskey. By the 1820s the government established a special police force to catch drunkards; the fines were extremely high. But these efforts did not curb drinking. The government levied higher taxes on whiskey production, which did decrease consumption, but unfortunately also tax revenues. Moreover, there continued to be numerous illegal producers of whiskey who did not pay these taxes. So the government decided to cut taxes on distilleries as a way to curb the illegal production of whiskey and to gain more tax revenues. As a result, many illegal distillers decided to become legal and pay taxes. Tax revenues did increase, although some illegal distilling remained. Ironically the government wanted to decrease working-class whiskey consumption, yet at the same time they relied on extensive alcohol taxes to balance the budget.

In addition to governmental efforts, temperance proponents in the nine-teenth-century also tried to convince the drinking public to moderate their consumption. These movements, which were predominantly Protestant, argued against drinking whiskey, purporting that wine, cider, or beer would be a better choice. Temperance literature claimed that excess whiskey use caused gout, kidney stones, cirrhosis of the liver, asthma, jaundice, poor eyesight, lack of sperm, barrenness in women, and infant mortality. Temperance writers felt they needed to warn drinkers of such extreme effects in order to compete with medical doctors who maintained that spirits could be useful as medicine. Some cur-rent authors argue, however, that rather than having public health in mind the temperance movements had the underlying purpose of controlling the Catho-lic majority in Ireland, who they believed to be the problem drinkers. Protestant temperance movements did further the culture of oppression toward the Catholic majority. Catholics, who made up 80 percent of the population, however, did not comply with the wishes of the temperance groups and continued to drink.

As the century wore on and the temperance strategy of focusing on personal moderation did not work, temperance groups changed their tactics. They worked toward legislative change instead, promoting Sunday closure laws, for example. The legislature did not cooperate with the temperance movements in this particular regard, however, because of the importance of alcohol taxes to the budget.

The Protestant temperance movements were joined by some Catholic tem-perance groups in the nineteenth-century, too. For these Catholic temperance groups, however, the impetus was to free Ireland from the rule of the British. Catholic nationalists believed that to win their freedom they must, among other things, focus on demonstrating a high moral character. One of the ways to do so was to curb alcohol consumption, since alcohol abuse and to some extent even consumption was equated with moral degeneracy. Many Catho-lics believed that England labeled Ireland as a country of drunkards in order to justify their political control of the country.

Temperance did seem to be successful in the long run in Ireland. A larger percentage of the population joined temperance movements in Ireland than did so in England or the United States. Moreover, the consumption levels of spirits by the Irish in the nineteenth-century were lower than that of the Americans. This pattern carried on into the twentieth-century as well. By the 1970s in Northern Ireland, for example, 34 percent of the population abstained, while in Britain only 9 percent abstained. So the stereotype of Irish drunkenness was overrated and perhaps was indeed a myth perpetuated by the British to maintain their power over Ireland.

France

Alcohol, in particular wine, shaped commerce, class, gender, international poli-tics, and government's role in society in eighteenth– and nineteenth–century

France. Wine was the de facto French national drink in the nineteenth-century. Industrialization of the wine trade was perhaps one of the most important areas of modernization, as attempts to broaden wine markets brought on the development of rail networks throughout the country. Moreover, the growth of wealth and the expansion of the industrial upper-class created a demand for fine wines, helping to define elite culture as far removed from that of the lower class. Public spaces serving alcohol also helped to define both gender and class identities. Cafés served both men and women unlike pubs in other Western countries, which served only men. As a result, French women were allowed a broader gender identity. At the same time, however, class specific venues perpetuated distinct differences in class cultures.

Moreover, wine, as emblematic not only of French trade but also of French identity, was used by the British to punish France. The British repeatedly cut off the wine trade with France. In response, the French made sure that wine quotas became central to international treaties with Britain as well as with other countries. Domestic regulation of alcohol in France focused on cafés, cabarets, and taverns. The government feared their role in precipitating rebellion because they were centers of French social life and daily gathering places for many.

Since wine was the predominant alcoholic drink in the eighteenth-century in France, far above beer or brandy, technological advancements centered around wine. In France scientific discoveries in wine spurred industrialization of the wine trade. Louis Pasteur, for example, discovered the best way to store wine for long periods of time: a narrow-necked bottle pointed down so no air could enter. Another chemist, Jean-Antoine-Claude Chaptal, made very important advancements in the production of wine, which also modernized the industry. He popularized using sugar in the process, stabilizing the wine and making it ferment faster. Sugar could also sweeten sour grapes and help make them into good wine. Even with these technological advancements, however, the disease of phylloxera seriously decimated the wine industry in France, as well as across Europe in the mid to late nineteenth-century. The European vines were not resistant to the infestation, and production of wine dropped by 60 to 90 percent. American vines, which were resistant because they had already had the disease, were grafted with the European vines and the vineyards began to recover.

Despite the phylloxera epidemic, the wine industry continued to modernize. Beginning in the 1850s the desire for larger wine markets helped to develop transportation networks to the wine-growing regions. Rail lines spread across the country to the grape-producing areas and helped to grow an internal market. Markets grew across Europe as well. For example, Germany, England, and the Netherlands imported large amounts of French wine. Some winemakers began to produce luxury wines for an increasingly wealthy subculture within France, making fine wine consumption a cultural characteristic of the upper-class. The majority of winemakers, though, mass produced cheaper wine for the lower-classes. During the nineteenth-century not only did wine making modernize, but distillation did as well. Even though industrial development in France lagged behind that of Britain, industrial distilleries remained vital, helping lead the way in French industrialization.

The burgeoning wine industry increasingly relied upon the proliferation of alcohol venues. Much like in other parts of the West the number of drinking establishments rose between the seventeenth- and nineteenth-centuries. For example, in Paris the number of drink shops grew from 3,000 in 1789 to over 30,000 in the late 1880s. The number of establishments across the country rose from approximately 100,000 in 1789 to 500,000 in 1914. One of the most popular drinking establishments was the café. There were different kinds of cafés, those that catered to the working-class, and several that catered to the upper-classes. Cafés were very important social centers for the French. They encompassed the space between private and public life, and exemplified the rise of leisure as a separate activity from work. Both men and women frequented cafés in France thus reflecting a more complicated gender ideology than the traditional nineteenth-century Western belief in the separation of women into the private sphere. Because they were divided by class, however, cafés did perpetuate class differences within France.

In addition to cafés, taverns, called cabarets, arose that catered to the working class. Much like in Britain and Ireland, urban, working-class men escaped from poor living conditions and joined other working-class men to drink and play games. Wine was most often the drink served in these taverns. Because these taverns served men of the same class, they, along with the cafés, helped solidify class boundaries. These taverns almost exclusively catered to men rather than women. If women drank in these taverns they were labeled as prostitutes, thus perpetuating a gender stereotype that automatically equated women's public alcohol consumption with loose morals.

The French also believed alcohol to be effective medically. Wine was used in several kinds of medicines. French doctors and their patients believed that a white wine mixed with juniper berries, squill, digitalis, and potassium acetate would cure heart disease. Wine was used for anemia, eczema, scurvy, and pneumonia. In 1898 Paris hospitals used over three million liters of wine in their cures. Louis Pasteur lauded the positive medicinal effects of wine so much so that in 1903 the French parliament voted to designate wine as healthy and hygienic. As newer more scientific medicines such as aspirin and antibiotics became popular, however, wine began to decline as an official medicine.

Personal alcohol consumption changed slightly in the nineteenth-century. Many in the lower-class in the north began to drink distilled spirits, or what they called "industrial spirits." Even with the increase in the consumption of spirits, though, wine continued to be the most popular alcoholic drink. The majority of peasants in the south of France continued to drink wine because most of the vineyards were located there and therefore wine was inexpensive. As the middle-class in France expanded, both their demand for commodities, as well as their desire to emulate the upper-class, led to an increase in their desire for quality wines. Fine wine consumption perpetuated growing consumerism and furthered the development of separate upper-, middle-, and working-class culture. Another elite commodity, champagne, also became a beverage popular with those in the middle-class who wanted to imitate upper-class lifestyles. The new consumer culture that demanded fine wine and champagne led to a boom in the alcohol advertising industry. For example, the 1855 Paris Exhibition advertised wines not only from France but also from places as far away as Australia. Champagne also became emblematic of the new advertising culture. The labels on the bottles depicted sports, romance, and patriotism – all ways to convince the buyer to consume the product.

Wine became a tool in international relations as well. The wine trade from France was so important that it became embroiled in the war between France and England in the early eighteenth-century. For example, as a result of the conflict, in 1703 the English closed their markets to French wines. French wine merchants, however, came up with alternative ways to get their product to the English consumer. Rod Phillips, author of *A Short History of Wine*, wrote that Bordeaux's wine merchants shipped their wine close to the English coast where English privateers then commandeered the wine, took it to England, and sold it. The privateers received most of the proceeds but likely shared them with the Bordeaux winemakers. There is no hard evidence to prove this theory, but since so much French wine continued to enter England, even though there was a ban on it, the story seems plausible. As the century progressed the wine trade continued to factor into international disagreements. As a result of ongoing tensions between France and England, in 1728 England banned bottled wine, only allowing the less stable barrel wine to be shipped into the country. This law hurt the French winemakers because by the time the barrel wine reached England its quality had deteriorated, thus decreasing French profits.

In the twentieth-century wine continued to be used in political battles. In the First World War the French military provided wine as part of the soldiers' rations during the fighting: they were given up to one liter of wine a day. After the war the French believed that the inclusion of wine in the war effort had helped lead to their success. Moreover, wine was included in international treaties in the twentieth-century. As noted in Rod Phillips' *Short History of Wine*, after the First World War, "the Treaty of Versailles required Germany to import 260,000 hectoliters of French wine each year free of tariffs." So throughout the modern period French wine played a noticeable role in international politics.

Unlike other Western countries in the nineteenth-century, the French government did not regulate drinking to such a great degree. Some attempts at alcohol regulation did exist, however. Temperance advocates in France believed industrial alcohol or spirits caused alcoholism, which was a "new" disease discovered in the mid-nineteenth-century. Moreover, in the late nineteenth-century, as fears of political uprisings grew during the Third Republic, the government increased repression of the café because it suspected cafés and cabarets of being centers of political rebellion. Therefore, nineteenth-century alcohol regulation in France focused on political repression of public spaces where drinking took place.

The United States

Alcohol in the nineteenth-century United States shaped the definitions of leisure, class, gender, and ethnicity. Alcohol consumption rose tremendously in the nineteenth-century. Much like in other industrializing countries, the rise in consumption resulted in part from the working class turning to alcohol to cope with the social upheaval of industrialization. Moreover, the proliferation of saloons facilitated the rise of drinking as the predominant form of leisure. Since most of these establishments catered to men only, and were segregated by class, they helped to define masculinity as well as to solidify working-, middle-, and elite-class boundaries.

Abuse of alcohol also rose in the nineteenth-century. In response, temperance groups spread across the country. Formed by Protestant churches, women, and the middle-class predominantly, these groups made up perhaps the most important reform movement of the era. They sought to "better" the working-class, especially the immigrant working-class, perpetuating ethnic and class prejudices. By the late nineteenth-century temperance groups began to lobby the government to legislate alcohol reform, attempting to co-opt the government into increasing regulations aimed at immigrants and the working-class.

After the turn of the century, temperance groups had succeeded, but like in most countries that tried to legislate prohibition, it did not work. Instead, prohibition led to organized crime, and some argue an increase in alcohol-related diseases. Furthermore, the government began to recognize that an influx of alcohol tax dollars could help bring the country out of the depression.

Industrialization in the United States revolutionized alcohol production. Mechanization of the beer industry in the nineteenth-century perpetuated an increase in the already growing alcohol consumption rates in the United States. In addition to a newly mechanized beer industry, European beer arrived in the United States with the mass immigration of Europeans, especially Germans. Germans brought lager beer to the United States where it began to be produced in the 1840s. By the 1870s lager beer became the most popular beer in the United States, subtly perpetuating cultural miscegenation. The industrialization of the beer industry spread even more rapidly in the late nineteenth century. For example, even though the population of the United States doubled during the period between 1880 and 1910, the production of beer increased four times. Two reasons for the tremendous increase in the production and distribution of beer were refrigeration and the national railroad system.

The number of saloons also rose in the nineteenth-century. By 1870 there were over 100,000 saloons across the country. Many of these saloons were tied to large breweries that came to dominate the industry. Because there were so many saloons, there was stiff competition among them, pushing them to attract customers through illegal activities such as gambling and prostitution.

The sale of alcohol also influenced the advertising industry in the nineteenth century. The alcohol industry began to rely on brand names to sell its products. Most of the advertising for alcohol promoted its health benefits. For example, "Doctor's Special Rum," "The Nourishing Ale," "Hall's Coca Wine," and "Barrett's Stout for invalids" were popularly advertised alcohols. Because the majority of the population was illiterate, advertising took the form of pictures of nurses on the bottles to illustrate their link to health. In addition, the official 1905 *Edition of the United States Pharmacopoeia* included wines and spirits as medicine. By 1916, however, influenced by the temperance movement, the Pharmacopoeial Convention deleted all alcohol from its contents, showing how politics could construct the definition of alcohol.

Along with increased production and trade of alcohol came increased consumption. The consumption of beer dramatically increased during the late nineteenth-century. While statistics from 1863 show that the average per capita consumption of beer was 1.7 gallons, by the 1910s that number had risen to 21 gallons. The growth in the number of saloons partly brought on this increase. Conversely, wine consumption did not rise along with beer. It constituted only 10 percent of the alcohol consumed in the nineteenth-century. Moreover, it tended to be used as medicine or in church ceremonies.

The rise in consumption made drinking the most popular pastime in the United States, defining leisure for many Americans. In agricultural settings before industrialization, people drank alcohol at various times during the day. Work was not separated from home and was bound by agricultural rhythms rather than the clock. During the transition to industrialization family members continued to bring buckets of beer to workers throughout the work day. As industry developed, however, businessmen no longer allowed their employees to drink on the job because of concerns about levels of production. As a result, men stopped by the corner saloon on their way to or from work to drink and socialize with each other. Drinking, then, helped to bracket work and leisure as distinct parts of one's day. The saloon became a focal point for male leisure, helping to create definitions of masculinity that coincided with the new industrial reality. Moreover, by excluding women, saloons perpetuated the stereotype that women who drank in public suffered from loose morals at best, and at worst were prostitutes. The rise of the saloon in the nineteenth-century also helped to shape urban neighborhoods. The corner saloon became a fixture in every urban working-class neighborhood. Furthermore, with the advent of the railroad, saloons appeared along rail routes at railroad stops, helping to define the nature of these stops as social settings rather than merely places to meet trains.

Many different kinds of saloons developed in the late nineteenth-century. Several saloons took out their seats to allow for more customers, forcing men to crowd along the bar, drink quicker, and consume more. In eastern cities many saloons catered almost exclusively to working-class, newly arrived immigrants. The marked increase in immigration by young, single men, especially from Ireland, increased the need for such saloons in their urban slums. Immigrant workers, however, were not the only ones who depended on saloons for leisure. Other groups in society, including the native-born working-class, middle-management, and capitalists all had saloons that catered to them in particular. Working-class saloons were by far the most numerous, however. All these saloons played a major role in solidifying class, gender, and ethnic boundaries in the industrializing United States.

Just as the numbers of saloons and the rates of beer consumption rose in the nineteenth-century, so did the demand for spirits. Statistics show that the consumption levels of spirits by 1830 were 300 percent higher than even those of the late twentieth-century – a highly developed consumer society. This sharp increase reflected the fact that Western grain farmers could more cheaply ship spirits than grain, and thus make more money. Two areas, the western United States and the eastern urban slums, were home to the heaviest consumers of spirits.

The increased use of both beer and spirits and the proliferation of drinking establishments went hand in hand with higher rates of abuse, which, in turn, provoked social and governmental regulation. Social movements aimed at regulating alcohol shaped the nature of nineteenth-century social reform in the United States. Some historians argue that temperance was the largest social movement in nineteenth-century America, larger than even abolition. Temperance movements became so popular that over 500,000 people in the United States pledged temperance or abstinence, and by 1830 over 1,000 temperance groups had been formed. Some temperance groups allowed for medicinal wine, although teetotaler movements did not.

Religious groups, especially the Quakers, were the first to publish anti-drinking tracts. Other religious groups also preached against the "evils" of drink. The American Temperance Society, dominated by evangelical Protestants who had been fired up by the Second Great Awakening, was the first national group. It was founded in Boston in 1826. The most well-known temperance organization was the WCTU or Women's Christian Temperance Union. It had national as well as international influence. The Presbyterian and Methodist Churches also became involved by issuing proclamations against drinking. Many churches at this time also switched to unfermented wine, or grape juice, in their ceremonies because of the temperance influence.

Apart from shaping social reform, temperance movements also influenced the cultural separation of the classes. By the mid nineteenth-century white, middle-class Protestants overwhelmingly supported temperance. They were concerned with the flood of immigration and the drinking habits of those immigrants from Ireland, Scotland, Germany, and later southern Europe. Some historians have argued that the alcohol issue was a way to curb any kind of political power that these new, working-class immigrants might aspire to.

Temperance strategies were numerous. Temperance movements early on urged the government to discontinue its ration to soldiers, and even limit the amount of alcohol soldiers could purchase. Temperance groups also founded temperance towns in many parts of the country, which prohibited drinking within their boundaries. For example, Prohibition Park, New York; Vineland, New Jersey; Harriman, Tennessee; Palo Alto, California; and Demorest, Georgia were all founded as temperance towns.

In the early to mid nineteenth-century the majority of the temperance organizations concentrated on the personal, moral aspects of abuse. Drinkers were seen as morally weak, criminal, or perhaps even insane. Temperance societies wanted to save the drunkard from his problems. Later in the century, however, temperance groups began to focus on prohibition legislation rather than working with the individual drinker. The Anti-Saloon League, a lobby group, put a great deal of pressure on legislatures to pass prohibition. By 1909 seven states had passed prohibition laws and by 1917 half of all of the states had passed prohibition. Seventy-five percent of the states had ratified the prohibition amendment by 1919, and by 1920 the Eighteenth Amendment went into law.

The Eighteenth Amendment legally stopped the "manufacture, sale or transportation of intoxicating liquors." (As quoted in Rothbaum *The Business of Spirits*.) It also had several unintended consequences. It increased organized crime. In fact, some argue that illegal sale of alcohol led to the rise of organized crime in the United States. Also, while some historians argue that prohibition did decrease the amount of alcohol people drank, others argue that it is difficult to know how much people did (or if they did) decrease their consumption because of large-scale bootlegging and the large number of illegal taverns called speakeasies. In some areas the number of bars even increased during prohibition. In New York City, for example, there were twice as many bars during prohibition as there were before prohibition – over 30,000. Moreover, the number of people who died from alcohol related diseases increased during prohibition as well.

By the early 1930s, however, people began to voice their opposition to prohibition. Many groups argued that it violated personal liberties, cost too much to enforce, and led to a big jump in crime, especially organized crime. The government also badly needed the tax revenue from alcohol because of the economic hardship brought on by the depression. Consequently, the Eighteenth Amendment was repealed in 1933. Ending prohibition and subsequently taxing alcohol played an important part in governmental attempts to end the depression.

After the end of prohibition, though, temperance movements did not disappear. One of the most successful social organizations in the twentieth and early twenty-first-centuries has been Alcoholics Anonymous. Rather than advocating for legislative reform, it has worked through meetings that promote the self-restraint of its members. Much like in the nineteenth-century, AA focused on the individual. In contrast to the nineteenth-century, however, it treated alcoholism as a disease rather than a moral failing. The majority in society in the late twentieth century, however, still did not believe in framing alcoholism as a disease.

African Americans and temperance

One of the things that set the United States apart from other Western countries in the nineteenth- and early twentieth-centuries was African slavery and its cultural aftermath. Since temperance was so central in the nineteenth-century, African American responses shed even more light on the role of alcohol in American culture. African Americans involved themselves in the temperance movement as well. Like Catholics in Ireland, many blacks believed that promoting temperance would decrease racism, or dispel the erroneous stereotype that black men were drunkards. In fact, American black temperance advocates were even invited to Ireland to lecture to groups of people on both temperance and abolition. Before emancipation, many free blacks, including leaders such as Frederick Douglass, preached temperance for slaves, infusing anti-alcohol sentiment into the abolition movement. These leaders argued that drinking among slaves dulled their desires for freedom, and thus worked against abolition, while abstinence among slaves would be an effective threat to slave owners. White slave owners also believed in abstinence, but for different reasons. They believed that inebriation among black slaves would lead to rebellion, and thus wanted to curb drinking among blacks. There is little evidence, however, that there were any problems with drunkenness among slaves.

During reconstruction the temperance movement in relation to race changed. Racism increased and the fear of drunken free blacks fed into a growing post-emancipation form of racism. The fear of alcohol consumption among blacks became a tool used during Jim Crow to support racism. In fact, the stereotype of African American alcohol abuse was used in many states to deny blacks their right to vote. African American temperance movements continued to argue against drinking after emancipation, but instead of blaming the drinker for alcohol problems, they blamed the system. Frederick Douglass argued that poverty, racism, and exploitation of the working class led to excessive drinking, rather than the other way around. He also argued that abstinence by free blacks would lead to social betterment. As blacks migrated to northern cities, however, they moved into African American urban communities that had their own, very popular, segregated alcohol leisure industry. So social drinking became a significant part of the cultural identity of northern blacks after the turn of the century. Temperance ideology and alcohol stereotypes, however, continued to influence definitions of race, ethnicity, and class in the United States into the twenty-first-century.

Japan

Two non-Western areas, Japan and Russia, industrialized later than Western countries, yet provide the best comparisons to Western industrialization. Called late-comer industrializers, these two areas also had to respond to changes in alcohol production, trade, consumption, and regulation.

Even though Japan developed industrially, and felt the infiltration of Western culture, it successfully held onto emblematic aspects of Japanese culture through maintaining ritualized drinking habits that structured both festivals and social occasions. Western alcohol, such as beer and wine, however, did flood into Japan with the proliferation of restaurants that accompanied industrialization, spreading Western culture to an elite segment of Japanese society.

In Japan during the Meiji period, 1868–1912, the most important alcoholic beverage was sake. Sake remained dominant during the industrializing period, and even with the rise of mass production, people still brewed sake at home. It was customary for people to drink home-brewed sake during festivals and ceremonial occasions, as drinking remained much more ritualized in Japan than it was in the West. For example, sake shaped marriage rituals. To signify a woman's move from her parents' to her husband's house she took a symbolic last drink of sake with her family before she left. Other ritualized drinking took place at dinner parties. The ritual required the host to offer one filled sake glass to a guest. After drinking the sake the guest would wash out the sake glass in a water basin and return the cup to the host. This went on throughout the dinner party with guest after guest, keeping to the tradition that one never served oneself.

As sake breweries sprang up in the cities people began to buy sake by the bottle and drink more at each sitting, which increased alcohol use. This pattern of heavier drinking spread to the countryside with the opening of village taverns. Moreover, as restaurants spread during the Meiji era, so did the availability of sake when people dined out. Western restaurants spread too. They, however, served beer and wine, which increased the popularity of these Western drinks and became a piece of the cultural Westernization that took place during Japanese industrialization. As a result of increased drinking there arose a Japanese Temperance Society in 1884, but it was not until 1922 that laws forbidding minors from drinking alcohol were enacted. Temperance did not have as much of an impact in Japan as it did in the West, however.

Russia

Alcohol in Russia structured social rituals, influenced medicine and bolstered both the economy and the government. Russians, especially Russian males, consumed large amounts of alcohol, making the alcohol trade one of the most profitable in nineteenth-century Russia. Numerous alcohol rituals structured Russian culture, and alcohol taxes during many decades in the nineteenth-century provided the vast majority of the government's budget. Abuse did lead to a half-hearted attempt at prohibition in the early twentieth-century, which failed because the new communist government could not survive without alcohol tax revenues and because the Russian people depended upon alcohol to structure many parts of their lives.

Vodka was the most important alcohol consumed in Russia during industrialization. Vodka comes from the Slavic word for water, which indicates how common it was in Russian culture. Vodka was introduced into Russian society in the sixteenth-century and continued to be society's preferred drink. Vodka was so popular that it accounted for over 20 per cent of all internal Russian trade in the nineteenth-century. Because it was such a widely desired commodity, its industrial production became an important aspect of industrialization in Russia. With its mass production, vodka consumption levels rose as well. In addition to its economic importance, vodka also played a central social and cultural role in Russian society. Births, deaths, marriages, and other important social occasions were marked with vodka. Russians also believed in the power of vodka to cure ills, using it in medicinal ways such as soaking one's aching feet or rubbing it on one's head for a headache.

The regulation of alcohol in Russia predominantly took the form of taxation. The Russian government relied upon vodka taxes, which provided nearly 10 percent of government revenues in the eighteenth-century, and by the nineteenth-century over 30 percent. Moreover, by the middle of the nineteenth-century, the Russian government was funding most and sometimes all defense spending through vodka excise taxes. In 1894 the government declared a monopoly on the sale of alcohol, indicating its value for the governmental budget. Abuse of vodka rose in the nineteenth-century as well, and by 1914 the Russian government instated prohibition. This lasted until 1923 but only covered the retail sale of alcohol. Alcohol could still be served in restaurants, so prohibition was not as all encompassing as it was in the United States for example. Even limited prohibition failed, however. Russians continued to illegally consume alcohol, and since the government suffered from a precipitous drop in tax revenues, it could no longer support prohibition.

Conclusion

Comparing alcohol across eighteenth- and nineteenth-century industrializing countries in the West and beyond illuminates commonalities brought on by industrialization, but also shows how culture in each society mediated the industrial influence. First, the mechanization of alcohol production and modernization of trade in Britain, France, the United States, and Russia made beer and distilled liquor available to a greater number of people and facilitated a change in the nature of leisure. More alcohol fed the growing demand by the working class, allowing them a social outlet and providing them with the most popular way to cope with the social upheavals of industrialization. Second, industrialization of the production of alcohol also facilitated the rise in consumption across several societies including Britain, Ireland, France, the United States, Japan, and Russia. Increased consumption led to higher rates of abuse, thus alcohol abuse became a significant cultural phenomenon associated with industrialization.

Third, pubs in Britain and Ireland, saloons in the United States, and cafés and cabarets in France all provided a public space to socialize away from home and work. These spaces led the way in solidifying the separation of work, home, and leisure. Fourth, class-based establishments in Britain, Ireland, France, and the United States helped to create distinct working-class, middle-class, and elite cultural identities in all those Western societies. Moreover, in the United

States ethnic prejudice and racism led several working-class saloons to cater mainly to immigrants, and drinking establishments in northern, urban, black neighborhoods to accommodate African Americans alone. Fifth, most of the drinking establishments in Britain, Ireland, and the United States served men and excluded women, creating new definitions of masculinity and indeed appropriate femininity in the industrial period. In contrast, however, in France the café catered to both men and women, which helped perpetuate a gender identity that was more expansive for women than in the other Western, industrializing countries.

While overall alcohol consumption habits changed during industrialization, some forms of alcohol use did not. First, across many societies alcohol continued to be consumed as medicine. In Britain, Ireland, France, the United States, and Russia alcohol remained a key ingredient in medicine as these societies still believed in its curative properties well into the twentieth-century. Second, in the non-Western society of Japan, traditional, ritual consumption practices persisted even in the face of industrialization and Western influence, allowing the Japanese to hold onto their culture in their daily practices.

The virtually universal rise in alcohol use accompanying industrialization brought on higher levels of abuse, which, in turn, led to more social and cultural problems that then gave rise to regulation by the state as well as civic groups. First, the pharmacological effects of spirits over that of fermented alcohol caused greater physical and social problems associated with abuse across many societies including Britain, Ireland, France, the United States, and Russia. Second, governments and reform movements across many societies including Great Britain, Ireland, and the United States mainly focused on abuse by the working-class and ethnic minorities. Reform movements provided a way for middle-class, white reformers to manage their fear of the increase in ethnic immigration and their need to socially control the growing working-class and the ethnically marginalized. Second, governments relied upon the alcohol taxes to make a measurable difference in their revenues. For many countries including Ireland, the United States, and Russia, alcohol taxes provided a significant percentage of all government income. Third, temperance movements were most prevalent in Protestant-dominated societies such as Britain, Ireland (dominated by the Protestant minority), and the United States, while in the non-Protestant societies of France, Japan, and Russia, temperance groups were not as strong during this period. The Protestant ideology of self-restraint fed temperance ideology, which sought to control the seemingly out-of-control drinker, usually belonging to the working-class. At the same time, however, some oppressed groups in societies, for example, Catholics in Ireland and African Americans in the United States, embraced temperance as a tool to prove their respectability to the rest of society. So temperance movements could be used as tools of the socially dominant to further racism and class prejudice, but could also be used as tools of the oppressed to combat prejudice.

Fourth, Western as well as non-Western countries instituted some form of prohibition in the early twentieth-century. Complete prohibition existed in the United States, while prohibition of the retail sale of alcohol existed in Russia. Britain and Japan passed laws barring minors from drinking, and France repressively regulated the café. Yet the centrality of alcohol to society thwarted prohibition efforts everywhere. Fifth, temperance groups in the West professed to care about the health and welfare of the working-classes, yet certain subtexts existed. For example, in France the government feared socialist political movements that arose in pubs and cafés; in Ireland the Protestant minority feared the Catholic majority; in the United States the middle-class feared an increase in political power of African Americans and immigrants; and in all areas capitalists desired more productive workers.

Industrialization in the eighteenth-, nineteenth-, and early twentieth-centuries modernized the alcohol industry. As a result, the new modes of production and trade led to both an increase and a change in the nature of consumption. Consumption patterns shaped leisure as well as class, gender, and ethnic identities. The increase in consumption brought about temperance, and in some cases prohibition, which failed, leading the way to increased acceptance of alcohol consumption in the twentieth-century.

Further reading

Antsie, F. 1877. *On the Uses of Wine in Health and Disease.* London: Macmillan.

Barrows, S. and R. Room. (eds.) 1991. *Drinking Behavior and Belief in Modern History.* Berkeley: University of California Press.

Duis, P. R. 1983. *The Saloon: Public Drinking in Chicago and Boston 1880–1920.* Urbana: University of Illinois Press.

"Ethnography, Alcohol, and South-Central European Societies." 1984. Special issue. *East European Quarterly.* 18 (4): 385–519.

Forbes, R. J. 1948. *Short History of the Art of Distillation: from the Beginnings up to the Death of Cellier Blumenthal.* Leiden: E. J. Brill.

Gordon, E. 1913. *The Anti-Alcohol Movement in Europe.* New York: Fleming H. Revell Company.

Gutzke, D. W. 2006. *Pubs and Progressives: Reinventing the Public House in England, 1896–1960.* Dekalb: Northern Illinois University Press.

Haine, W. S. 1996. *The World of the Paris Café, Sociability Among the French Working Class, 1789–1914.* Baltimore, MD: Johns Hopkins University Press.

Kunio, Y. 1957. *Japanese Manners and Customs in the Meiji Era.* Trans. C. S. Terry. Tokyo: Obunsha.

Malcolm, E. 1986. "Ireland Sober, Ireland Free." In *Drink and Temperance in Nineteenth-Century Ireland.* Syracuse: Syracuse University Press.

Mehta, J. N. n.d. *Alcohol and State Revenue.* New Delhi: All India Prohibition Council.

Okrent, D. 2010. *Last Call: The Rise and Fall of Prohibition.* New York: Scribner.

Phillips, R. 2000. *A Short History of Wine.* New York: Harper Collins.

Rumbarger, J. J. 1989. *Profits, Power, and Prohibition: Alcohol Reform and the Industrializing of America, 1800–1930.* Albany: State University of New York Press.

Watney, J. 1974. *Beer is Best: A History of Beer.* London: Peter Owen.

6 Imperialism and alcohol in the nineteenth- and early twentieth-centuries

The second great wave of colonialism in the eighteenth- and nineteenth-centuries changed the world's political map, especially in Africa, South Asia, and Australia. Industrialization and attendant technological advances in the West facilitated nineteenth-century colonialism. European countries including Britain, France, the Netherlands, Germany, and Belgium all divided up the continent of Africa under their own flags. Most of Africa was colonized in the late nineteenth-century and did not become independent countries until the mid-twentieth century. As an exception, South Africa became independent much earlier than most African countries but remained under oppressive white minority rule until the end of the twentieth-century. On another continent the British began to consolidate their rule in India in the 1700s, which lasted until that country's independence in 1947. In yet another part of the world the British colonized Australia in the eighteenth-century and colonization there lasted until 1901 when Australia became a commonwealth. Colonialism radically changed the lives of the indigenous people in Africa, India, and Australia. In respect to alcohol, new kinds of alcohols began to be produced in the colonies while traditional, indigenous beers continued to be made. The international alcohol trade grew and the alcohol trade within the colonies increased exponentially, which brought great wealth to some and serious social problems to others. Consumption of alcohol both by the colonizers and serious the colonized skyrocketed, resulting in regulations that became one of the tools used by governments to oppress indigenous populations in these colonized areas.

Africa

The very diverse African continent was home to many different modes of alcohol production, trade, consumption, and regulation during the colonial period. Yet similar experiences characterized many cultures. Alcohol structured the lives of native Africans. It anchored their belief systems, sometimes providing the most visible way to retain their native culture in the face of colonialism. Alcohol set in motion work parties, brought together families in marriage, maintained social hierarchies, and defined the daily African diet. Alcohol production constructed gender identity; in most areas of Africa women exclusively made beer, and in other societies only men controlled that task.

As the Europeans infiltrated Africa, alcohol consumption rose. The colonists socialized in white only pubs, publicly setting them apart from and demonstrating their racial superiority to native Africans. The large public works projects such as mining brought together thousands of native laborers, creating a high demand for alcohol. As a result, indigenous women beermakers earned their own money selling to the miners, gaining economic independence from their husbands and upsetting traditional gender roles. In growing urban areas alcohol also defined society's idea of appropriate gender roles. Women's public consumption of alcohol now labeled them as loose or even as prostitutes. The change in alcohol patterns not only disrupted women's roles, but it also upset the male social hierarchy. Young men earned money in the new economy, which gave them access to alcohol, a culturally significant good that had been strictly controlled by elders. Moreover, alcohol ushered in Westernization as native African men began to drink Western beer in pubs as a new form of leisure.

Native African leaders saw new patterns of alcohol consumption as a powerful symbol of colonialism, and as a major cause of the social disintegration that plagued the indigenous populations. They tried, mostly in vain, to regulate it. Colonial governments, however, were lukewarm at best to the kind of alcohol regulations that would result in fewer taxes, since in many colonies alcohol taxes were the largest contributor to their budgets. White controlled governments used alcohol as a powerful tool to subjugate black Africans. The highly regulated black–only beer hall system in South Africa was widely recognized as a pillar of apartheid. It is not surprising, then, that control over alcohol became a major component of many independence movements across the continent.

The production of beer in Africa was so central to native cultures that Africans embedded it in their mythology. Kofyar legends from Nigeria, for example, related that their mythical cultural hero founded villages in the places where he stopped to brew beer. The actual production of beer in Africa goes back millennia. Africans in Western and Southern Africa used two staple grain, millet and sorghum to produce beer. Much later when colonists arrived and began growing a particular kind of corn, or a variety of sorghum, it became an important staple in the production of beer. Keith H. Steinkraus in *Fermented Food Beverages in Nutrition* describes the entire process of making this beer. One first steeped the grain for six to 36 hours, then germinated it by laying it out for four to six days while periodically moistening it. Next the grain was dried in the sun. The producer then made a mash of it by putting it in hot water, which caused it to sour. The mixture was then boiled. Malt was added and then the beer was cooled. It was ready in four to eight hours. Across Africa people brewed beer in similar ways, using a variety of ingredients, and in each area beer provided an important nutritional staple as well as a way to mark social and ceremonial events.

In most areas in Africa women brewed beer. In Zambia, for example, women brewed many types of traditional beers. Women brewed "work beer" for work parties that cleared trees, prepared gardens, weeded, built houses, or thatched roofs. Women also prepared "ceremonial beer" for important transitions in life such as births and deaths. Immediately after death women brewed "first beer". It symbolically cleansed the relatives of the pollution from their contact with the dead. Women then prepared a "second beer" three months after the death. It served to pay respect to the deceased and to determine inheritance. If harvests were bad and beer was in short supply, women might make "secret beer" for a privileged elder of the village who asked for it. Finally, women made "political beer". Those running for office sent this beer around to village leaders in order to garner support. Beer production gave women an essential role in the social, cultural, and political life of the village.

In Tanzania men made beer. Banana beer was the staple beer in this area. Men made banana beer from a particular kind of banana that was ripened by hanging it upside down over the hearth, or burying it in the ground for several days. During that time the fermentation process began. Later, men placed the bananas in dug-out wooden troughs with dried grasses and stomped on them in order to make a mash. The beer makers then added dried sorghum to the mixture, covered it in banana leaves, and left it to ferment for 24 hours. The beer was then ready to drink. Beer making in Tanzania as well as across Africa was a basic responsibility in villages because beer was essential to diets and cultural practices. Therefore, gender-specific production of beer, like in Zambia and Tanzania, helped to define masculine and feminine gender roles. Whoever produced beer not only fed the community, but also reproduced one of society's vital pieces of material culture.

Alcohol as an international trade item dated back to the first interactions between Africans and Europeans. During the 300 years of the Atlantic slave trade European alcohol purchased a significant percentage of those Africans sold into slavery. Alcohol became an even more valuable trade item between Africa and the West during the African colonial period, between the late nineteenth-century and the middle of the twentieth-century. Along with guns, alcohol was one of the commodities that the West, particularly the British, traded for raw materials in Western Africa. African raw materials garnered from the alcohol trade helped further the industrial revolution in the West. Furthermore, the alcohol industry in Western Europe depended upon the colonial markets in Africa in order to survive.

As demand for alcohol in Africa increased during the colonial period, more alcohol began to be produced in the colonies, and sold especially to the colonists. Moreover, alcohol venues, for both domestic and imported alcohol, proliferated. In Angola, for example, alcohol sales provided entrepreneurial opportunities for many colonists. European merchants opened taverns and quickly became rich as a result. Immigrants drank large quantities of alcohol because these taverns were practically the only leisure establishments available for the Angolan settlers. Taverns became so numerous in the nineteenth-century that in Luanda there was a tavern for every 34 inhabitants. In Zambia, like Angola, the alcohol trade exploded. The settlers in Zambia drank copious amounts of alcohol in pubs. In Angola and Zambia, like in many other areas in Africa, alcohol consumption in public establishments became the predominant symbol of leisure for the colonists, mimicking patterns in the industrializing West.

Native Africans, too, were affected by alcohol in the cash economy. In the gold mines of South Africa alcohol itself became currency. The mine owners often paid African workers with domestically produced alcohol. It gave the Boer settlers a market for their grain and provided a cheap way to pay the miners. Using alcohol as pay drastically increased alcohol use by the miners and decreased the amount of income they could bring home to their families, thus hurting their relationships with their families and villages. For many South African miners alcohol shaped their experience in the market economy.

The sizeable increase in demand for alcohol led to the commodification of indigenous beer. In many regions women were the primary producers of beer, so they used their skills to move into the market economy. Therefore, in addition to making beer for ceremonial and social events, they began to make beer to sell. Women had this opportunity particularly in mining areas in South Africa where large populations of single men had currency to buy beer. As women made money they no longer had to depend upon their husbands, who, in many cases, had numerous wives also vying for support. Women spent their newfound earnings on their children. For example, they sent their children to school, influencing the next generation of Africans. Women's involvement in alcohol sales not only allowed their independence from their husbands, but also changed levels of literacy in Africa, especially among girls.

In Zambia, like in South Africa, brewing beer became a way for women to make money. Women sold beer to the locals or to those traveling through the newly constructed roads leading to the mines. Much of their locally produced beer was sold out of taverns called "shebeens." These small, makeshift bars were in a woman's own home, and accounted for most of the alcohol sales in rural areas. Alcohol brought in more revenue than food or other items because it was so popular among the men who were now earning money as wage laborers. Women's economic independence in many areas in Africa rested upon their ability to sell alcohol for money.

Many Africans consumed beer for nutritional reasons. Indigenous beer remained an important dietary supplement for native Africans. For example, sorghum beer augmented the diets of many rural South Africans, especially the lower class. Workmen drank as much as five pints per day. Thirty-five percent of a worker's calories came from locally made beer. The beer contained important nutrients such as thiamine, riboflavin, and nicotinic acid. Even infants in South Africa were fed the dregs of the beer, which contained nutrients as well. In southern Nigeria millions of people continued to drink indigenous alcohol as part of their diets. People drank at least half a liter per day of palm wine because it was such an important part of their nutritional intake. Half a liter contained over 300 calories, vitamins, protein, riboflavin, and vitamin B. In Tanzania, daily moderate consumption of banana beer was considered essential to a balanced diet and was even thought to bring on sexual potency in men. Alcohol as food helped make possible the survival of tens of thousands of Africans.

During colonization the consumption of alcohol by indigenous Africans rose dramatically, however. In Zambia, traditional beer called chibuku began to be mass produced, and along with the proliferation of municipal taverns caused an escalation in drinking. Now strangers were more likely to drink together in taverns, and binge drinking became more common, which many times led to fights. Moreover, new kinds of more potent alcohol, spirits, were introduced in many areas of Africa and thus made intoxication easier. The habit of drinking for leisure by indigenous Africans increased the amounts and frequency of their drinking. As a result, the abuse of alcohol escalated. Many authors argue that alcohol consumption increased during the colonial period because Africans used alcohol as a means of escape from the tremendous social upheaval that colonialism caused in the society.

Not only did an increase in consumption of alcohol by indigenous Africans occur, but also the demographics of those who drank alcohol changed. As young men moved into the cash economy in urban areas they now had more access to alcohol because they could use their earnings to buy it. Moreover, with the mass production of beer, many young men began to drink bottled instead of indigenous beer because it signified one's entrance into the middle class and independence from the male elders in one's home village. In southern Ghana, for example, prior to colonization, male elders controlled the distribution and consumption of palm wine, the primary alcoholic drink and a symbolically powerful example of material culture. Palm wine was essential in many ritual and ceremonial activities within the culture. Elders controlled the land on which the palms grew, and most importantly, they controlled the culturally powerful alcohol produced from it that brought access to women.

Once young men in the villages began to have their own money after migrating to the gold coast to work in the cash economy, they increasingly balked at village rules and began to drink in public for leisure. They were able to challenge the power of the elders in a profound way through their ability to buy and consume alcohol. Moreover, most of the young males migrated only temporarily to the city and then returned to their rural homes with enough capital to buy their own land, and therefore control their own access to alcohol and women. Their ability to consume such a symbolically powerful commodity of their own accord severely weakened the power of the male elders. This generational change in access to alcohol helped to rupture the traditional male social hierarchy in Southern Ghana.

Unlike men, women did not have the option of buying and publicly consuming alcohol for the sake of leisure. Just as in many Western societies if women drank in commercial establishments society assumed they were prostitutes. Husbands and wives rarely drank together in public because it was commonly assumed that when men went out to drink they were often looking for extra-marital sex. Westernization brought with it leisure in the form of drinking in public establishments. Public leisure drinking by men solidified the connection between alcohol and women's socially unacceptable sexual conduct, effectively curtailing women's freedom in urban Africa.

Not all African culture was dominated by Western concepts of alcohol and leisure in the cash economy. In rural Western Africa, for example, the Kofyar, who were farmers in northern Nigeria, continued to define much of their social and spiritual life through the use of beer. In eastern Africa the Iteso tribe of Kenya continued to use alcohol in ritual and ceremonial ways, and in Tanzania, the rural Haya people of the Lesser Kyamutwara Kingdom continued to use banana beer for social and religious purposes. These groups and many more like them continued to use beer as a medium to frame their cultural practices. Many vital and social customs depended upon the use of beer. First and foremost beer remained indispensable for ancestor worship and funeral ceremonies. Second, beer continued to strengthen social, family, and gender hierarchies within villages. Third, beer prevailed as currency in tribute practices, and finally it continued to structure marriage and family ceremonies.

Ritual use of beer dominated the practice of ancestor worship in many African societies. In Nigeria, for example, descendents broke beer jars and blew beer over the graves of their ancestors. In Tanzania every man had to offer beer to the alter of his deceased father before drinking it himself. Moreover, the head of the family offered banana beer to the ancestors in return for the health of his family and the fertility of his wife or wives. Even the king in Tanzanian society ritually provided banana beer to the ancestors. In Zambia a critical rite of passage for a newly married woman included making and then offering to make beer for her husband's and her own ancestors, furthermore during any kind of ritual drinking people offered beer to the spirits before they drank it themselves. In funeral rituals in Zambia an appointed person took a sip of homemade beer in front of the entire village, spit it on the grave, and prayed to the spirit of the deceased for the well-being of the village. All of these societies depended upon beer to shape the most significant of ceremonies in their cultures, those that honored the dead. The Iteso tribe in Kenya gave their deceased five funerals over a period of many years, with beer as a central ingredient in those ceremonies.

Indigenous beer also played a key role in solidifying social hierarchies within the village, the family, and between men and women. In Tanzania a village member, usually the village leader, obligatorily provided banana beer at festivals in exchange for the loyalty of others in the community, reinforcing the village hierarchy. The king of the Asante people in what is now Ghana supplied free alcohol to his people as they celebrated the Odwira festival. The hierarchy in Asante society was loosened because slaves and women drank freely. At the end of the festival, however, social order returned and the elders regained control over who had access to alcohol. The temporary suspension of drinking protocol sanctioned by the elite served to reinforce the normally strict social hierarchy within the kingdom by highlighting the exeptionalism of the festival. Ceremonial alcohol use was one of the predominant ways to keep social hierarchies in balance.

Family, generational, and gender hierarchies were reinforced with the ceremonial consumption of beer. In the Iteso tribe in Kenya families reinforced family hierarchies by drinking beer together. The family sat together around a communal vessel, each with a specifically defined place, and drank beer from shared straws in a predetermined order. When families entertained kin they also had to sit in specific places. Parents and children of the hosts sat on the right side, while grandparents, grandchildren, siblings, and the hosts sat on the left side. In addition, one could not share drinking straws with one's parents-in-law, unless the wife had prepared the beer specifically for her father-in-law and he then asked her to drink first. In Tanzania every man who made banana beer had to offer the first drink of that beer to his father. Generational hierarchies were reinforced through rules surrounding drinking as well. In Kenya, the Iteso tribe demonstrated the high respect paid to elders of the village by the practice of allowing elders to drink beer whenever and wherever they wished. Drinking practices solidified gender differences in many parts of rural Africa, too. In Tanzania, for example, men commonly drank beer out of long-necked calabashes using a reed straw, while women were only allowed to drink beer out of short-necked calabashes and were not allowed to use a straw. All of these highly ritualized customs demonstrated alcohol's crucial role in maintaining social order within communities across Africa.

In many parts of rural Africa the high value of beer made it a kind of currency. In South Africa, for example, within native villages, beer was used to gather work parties for individual or community projects. More workers could be convinced to help when alcohol was the reward, rather than when food was offered. In Nigeria villages paid medicine men with beer. And in Tanzania kings were given beer as tribute. Beer as currency even for kings reflects its status in rural societies in Africa.

Beer also was a vital part of marriage ceremonies and other family rituals. In Zambia, the bride and groom's relatives both poured beer at the entryway to the couple's house to symbolize the coming together of the two lineages, as well as the joining of "field" and "hearth". In Tanzania the exchange of banana beer was expected during marriage negotiations between families. In another family ceremony beer was used to choose a baby's name in the Iteso tribe in Kenya. The family chose a name and then the grandmother tested out the name by offering beer on her finger to the baby. If the baby drank the beer, the chosen name was accepted. If the baby rejected the beer, the process started again. Families depended upon the symbolic power of beer to give power to their important rites of passage. In all of these ways, ancestor worship, social and family hierarchy reinforcement, tribute, and marriage and family rituals, Africans used beer to hold onto their culture in the face of colonialism.

Although traditional patterns of alcohol use persisted in many rural areas, overall drinking increased tremendously across Africa, and, as a result, regulation followed. Africans themselves tried to have the importation of alcohol banned. At the Berlin Conference in 1884 and again at the 1889 Brussels Conference, African leaders lobbied for a ban on alcohol trafficking. At the 1889 conference both the importation of European alcohol as well as the indigenous distillation of alcohol were banned between the parallels of 20 degrees north and 22 degrees south. During the Sixth International Congress on Alcohol Abuse in Brussels in 1897, Bishop Oluwole, representing Nigeria, argued that the importation of spirits was crippling Nigeria. He wanted Nigeria to begin to import more useful items for the development of the country. He argued that alcohol increased crime and brought other social problems to the capital, Lagos. These regulations on alcohol strove to keep native Africans, not European settlers, from drinking. The international community realized the powerful effect alcohol was having on the African people.

The concern over alcohol abuse by native Africans was so widespread that it became one of the major topics in the Peace Accords following the First World War. One of the agreements in 1919 regulated the liquor trade in Africa, both the international trade as well as the manufacture of alcohol in the colonies. The treaty, signed at St. Germain-en-Laye in 1919, prohibited "the importation, trade, and possession of trade spirits of every kind and beverages mixed with these spirits in the entire African continent with the exception of some countries in North Africa and the Union of South Africa." (From Marcus Grant *Alcohol and Emerging Markets: Patterns, Problems, and Responses*.) International leaders chose to control the influx of alcohol into Africa because they recognized the power it had to disrupt the social and political stability on the continent as well as ruin the lives of those who abused it. While perhaps well meaning, alcohol regulations fostered the strict racial hierarchy that developed with colonialism across Africa because these laws were aimed at the native population.

International agreements aside, the colonial governments themselves were ambivalent about the alcohol trade. On the one hand, they gained considerable income from taxes, tariffs, and licenses, on the other hand, however, they, along with Christian missionaries, wanted to control the consumption habits of native Africans. In colonial Nigeria, for example, liquor taxes provided the bulk of the fiscal support for the colonial government, up to 75 percent. Many in Nigeria believed there to be serious problems with alcohol abuse, however. In South Africa early policies allowed for miners to be paid in alcohol as an incentive to continue working in the mines. White South Africans, however, began to believe that alcohol consumption by the workers lowered worker productivity. As a result, in 1897 the government prohibited blacks from drinking alcohol. Some capitalists, however, wanted to be able to entice workers with the promise of alcohol. Consequently, the government passed a law in 1898 allowing native Africans to drink, but only if they were working for a white employer. This law gave whites much more control over the labor of the blacks, the majority of whom wanted to be able to drink. Furthermore, in 1908 the government formed a monopoly on beer, creating a highly regulated beerhall system. Beerhalls became the only legal place where black Africans could drink. High barbed wire fences surrounded many of these beerhalls and native South Africans likened the experience to "drinking in a cage." Moreover, the beer was much more expensive than homemade beer, thus a higher percentage of workers' incomes went to alcohol and not to family necessities.

The beerhalls came to be the preeminent representation of the racist policies of the government. Therefore, rioting against the beerhalls became a direct affront against the government. And people did riot. Not only did they riot, but they also successfully boycotted the beerhalls. In 1929 a year-long boycott by one of the unions caused the government to lose significant income. By mid century the beerhalls were one of the major symbols of apartheid, so much so that in 1976 during anti-apartheid riots many beerhalls were burnt to the ground. Women, especially, rioted against the beerhall system because of the tremendous loss of income they caused. The beerhalls competed with their primary form of livelihood, selling alcohol out of small storefronts connected to their homes.

Eliminating the "shebeens," or the outlets for homemade beer run by women, became another strategy for controlling indigenous alcohol consumption. Women continued to make and sell beer, however, even in the face of continuous raids by the South African police. Many raids on shebeens turned violent. Officials saw their very existence as a major affront to the government. During one raid in 1960 nine policemen were killed and as a result the government outlawed the ANC (African National Congress), the most important bulwark against apartheid. The illegal manufacture and sale of liquor by women in shebeens became a major political statement against the repressive practices of the government. Control over the consumption of alcohol became one of the symbols of freedom by black South Africans.

In Zambia, like in South Africa, the government believed that native Africans needed to be controlled, and they limited access to alcohol to do so. The colonial rulers believed that Africans were prone to drunkenness and unruly behavior, particularly sexually, and thus needed extra rules regarding liquor – especially spirits. In 1930 the Native Beer Ordinance, or the Traditional Beer Act, regulated both where and what native Zambians could drink. The colonial government made it illegal for native Africans to drink any beverage other than home-brewed beer. Moreover, the government prohibited native Africans from making home-brewed beer in urban areas. Instead, the government took over the production of homebrew in the cities, tightening their hold over alcohol even more. Furthermore, the government began to require women who made beer in rural areas to buy special permits. In the cities the government established beerhalls. These beerhalls were meant to control drinking particularly by copper miners who lived in dorms while working in the mines. Away from their families, and with some disposable income, the miners wanted to spend their leisure time drinking. The government, however, sought to extend their control over the miners by regulating their free time. Control over drinking embodied the oppressive racial policies of the colonial government in Zambia.

As nationalist movements rose after the Second World War, however, Zambians began to fight for more autonomy over their own alcohol consumption. The African Representative Council, which was formed in 1946, gave Zambians the right to vote on issues surrounding alcohol. Zambians voted that they should be able to buy European bottled beer and wine. The government implemented the new regulations within two years. Not all laws changed, however. Whites still did not allow "mixed" drinking, which was drinking by blacks and whites in the same place; the women who traditionally made beer still did not have the right to make and sell beer where they pleased; and finally, the hated beerhalls still existed. The changes had made only small steps toward more freedom for Zambians.

The ability to choose what and where they drank was only part of the movement toward personal independence for Zambians. Zambian women fought the colonial government to regain their traditional place as beer producers. Beer making was central to their identity and economic independence. As a result, they created one of the largest pre-independence demonstrations in Zambia, the 1954 beer riots. "More than two thousand women were involved, many with babies on their backs; they were tear-gassed and clubbed by the police for protesting the regulations that prohibited brewing and sale in towns." (In Alan Haworth "Zambia" in *International Handbook on Alcohol and Culture.*) Even after Zambian independence in 1964, however, women still did not have the right to brew and sell traditional beers in town. The new government closed the hated beerhalls, yet ironically, men set up "tea rooms" that sold beer, again usurping the power of Zambian women. Colonization had set in motion the appropriation of traditional power enjoyed by Zambian women. Alcohol production was central to that power. Even after independence the vestiges of colonialism remained in the form of gender bias against women selling alcohol.

Much like similar laws in South Africa and Zambia, the colonial government of Nigeria formulated policies to control alcohol. In 1920 it instated high duties on the alcohol trade and a licensing system for alcohol outlets. Next it called for prohibition in some parts of Nigeria, particularly in the Muslim north. Furthermore, in public establishments the government tried to substitute light beer for the imported high-alcohol spirits. Finally, the government wanted to control the tapping of oil-palm trees used to make palm wine, and to prohibit local distillation of spirits. The government aimed these directives at native Nigerians in an attempt to further control their behavior. These rules lasted until the Second World War when the government legalized the distillation and sale of local alcohol in response to growing nationalist movements. The nationalists subsequently took control of the alcohol trade, which they saw as a major symbol of independence.

In Ghana, indigenous leaders and the British colonial authorities vied for control of alcohol. Alcohol policy became a central bargaining piece between the two groups in their constant negotiations over the extent of colonial rule. Chiefs and other elders concurred with the colonial government that alcohol needed to be regulated, but for two very different reasons. The elders were particularly concerned with the increased availability of it to young men. The availability caused an upheaval in the social order in the villages because young men had previously had little power over their own alcohol consumption. Yet with their move into the market economy they were able to buy their own alcohol without permission from the elders. The government allowed the tribal chiefs some control over access to liquor by younger men as long as the government continued to earn tax revenues from the liquor trade. In this way the goals of the elders, to maintain the social hierarchy, dovetailed with the goals of the colonial government, to profit from the liquor trade. Nevertheless, the elders eventually lost their power. The colonial government still profited from alcohol sales to younger, wealthier men, however.

Some of the largest tax revenues came from the liquor trade in Ghana. In fact, alcohol taxes became crucial to the success of the British colonial government there. To boost tax revenues, the colonial government even allowed an increase in the number of liquor establishments. Ironically, these establishments became centers for political unrest as nationalist groups began agitating for independence. The liquor trade in Ghana financially propped up the colonial government on the one hand, while, on the other hand, alcohol venues became centers for organizations that led to the government's eventual downfall.

India

Colonial India witnessed skyrocketing alcohol consumption as the British brought both their alcohol and their drinking habits with them to the continent. Drinking alcohol, especially Western alcohol, became a symbol of Westernization for middle- and upper-class Indians. While native leaders voiced their concerns regarding rising consumption rates, the colonial government heavily relied on alcohol taxes to fund its treasury. As a result, the nationalist movements toward the end of the nineteenth- and beginning of the twentieth-centuries saw temperance, even abstinence, as a hallmark of the rejection of British rule. Unfortunately, alcohol had become such a central feature of Indian life as a status symbol for the rich, and as a crucial revenue for the independent governments, that its attempted prohibition failed.

The British introduced Scotch whiskey to India during the early colonial period. Drinking it became a status symbol for the rich and Westernized. Western drinking habits became a potent symbol of the British ability to infuse Western culture into the Indian subcontinent and a repudiation of Muslim and Vedic Hindu traditions. Middle-class Indians who were enamored of the British, especially those who were educated in the colonial system, began to drink more alcohol in general. As a result, Indian importation of alcohol increased by 900 percent between 1875 and 1928. The trade in liquors increased so much so that by the late nineteenth-century every village market had a designated space for the sale of spirits.

The British government regulated the skyrocketing trade in alcohol through taxes. When the British gained power in India they promoted the production and trade of liquor because of the profitable tax revenues. In 1773 the state monopolized the liquor trade and by 1790 the state had added an excessive excise tax on alcohol. These high taxes resulted in two outcomes desired by the British: considerably more tax revenues, which they depended upon to run the government, and high liquor prices, which discouraged drinking by all but the upper classes. Throughout the colonial period drinking continued to increase, and between 1891 and 1930 tax revenues on alcohol rose by 800 percent. Throughout the colonial period alcohol taxes made up a sizeable proportion of governmental revenues and contributed in a substantial way to the success of the colonial project.

While the government enjoyed high tax revenues from the alcohol trade, social reformers worried about problems that resulted from alcohol abuse. Both Hindu and Muslim reformists demanded the total abolition of some spirits. Not only did alcohol reform movements have indigenous roots, but they also were influenced by the popular temperance movements in Britain in the late nineteenth-century. In response to such widespread reactions against drinking, the government adopted the policy of restricting the production and importation of some spirits and continued to raise taxes to deter alcohol consumption among the majority of the population, the poor. Reformers were joined by nationalist movements in their concern over alcohol abuse. The Indian National Congress, which was founded in 1885, passed resolutions against excessive alcohol consumption. Its members argued that the British did not have an adequate temperance program in India. Thus the prohibition campaign became central to the platform of the Indian National Congress. In addition, Ghandi, who believed in abstinence, championed the prohibition cause. Ghandi said he believed "drink to be more damnable than thieving and perhaps even prostitution." Alcohol regulation, then, became a cornerstone of the Indian independence movement.

After independence in 1947, India added prohibition to its 1950 constitution. It said "the state shall endeavor to bring about prohibition of the consumption, except for medical purposes, of intoxicating drinks and drugs which are injurious to health." (As quoted in Marcus Grant, *Alcohol and Emerging Markets: Patterns, Problems, and Responses.*) It was up to the individual states to enforce prohibition, however, which was difficult because they had to deal with rampant smuggling. In addition, it was not easy to enforce prohibition with elites who still viewed drinking as a status symbol. Moreover, the states that did enforce prohibition suffered because they lost substantial tax monies, so many states ended it as a result. By the late 1970s most Indian states had outlawed prohibition, mainly because of the loss to their tax revenues. Prohibition as a national cause had come to an end. The realities of state budgets offset any prohibitionist sentiments. For India, alcohol had been significant in many ways. It brought in essential taxes to the colonial government, shaped the platform of the independence movement, and provided indispensible tax revenues to the post-independence Indian government.

Australia

The history of Australia differs dramatically from that of India, even though both were British colonies. Australia started out as a penal colony in the late eighteenth-century, drawing mostly men rather than women to the continent. The indigenous population was quite small, and much of the research on drinking habits and laws have focused on the white immigrant population.

Colonists brought a distinct alcohol culture to Australia, one that has defined national identity into the twenty-first-century. Early on, the British elites consciously separated themselves from the rest of society through their taste for wine and love of viticulture. Pubs, however, became the hallmark of Australian society. Pubs, more so than any other institution, staked out colonial settlements as white society spread inland, defining white life in Australia and bringing Western culture to the interior. Moreover, pubs opened up new gender roles for women who were allowed, even encouraged, to become barmaids, thus separating gender identity in Australian society from that of Europe where women had already been pushed out of the occupation. Pub culture also defined masculinity in Australia, bestowing it on the white men who alone frequented the establishments and emasculating the aboriginal men who were barred. Furthermore, pubs became de facto centers of political power, where white men made virtually all the political decisions excluding women and aborigines from the right to a national identity. Pubs symbolized such power in Australia that the right to finally enter them meant as much to aboriginal and women's rights movements as their eventual right to vote.

Colonization brought viticulture to Australia. The first attempt at producing wine by prisoners came in 1801. It did not turn out well. It was not until a little over a decade later that wine production began to flourish. Several well-known male colonists began to promote viticulture, and by the 1830s Australian wine had made its way to Europe where it was well received. In fact, in many French competitions Australian wine won high marks, much to the chagrin of the French judges who believed the best wine to be from France. Even though wine production continued to develop in Australia, it was not a common drink among the majority of the population. Most colonists, especially the lower classes, imbibed in beer and spirits. The elite minority of the British preferred wine, seeing it as more refined. As a result, wine consumption became a way to separate elite culture from that of the lower-classes in Australian society.

Trade in alcohol became central to the economy and culture in Australia, and pubs were the main outlets for that trade. Pubs were on the forefront of colonization. Pubs carried both the British Empire and British culture to Australia. Before churches or other public buildings, pubs staked out new territory for colonization. As Diane Kirkby wrote in *Barmaids: A History of Women's Work in Pubs* "Pubkeeping had a central place in the process of colonisation." Especially with the discovery of gold in many places in Australia, pubs followed gold miners into the wilderness. Pubs also provided self-employment, especially for women. Even though pub keeping was no longer the purview of women in England, it was in the colony of New South Wales. By the end of the nineteenth-century women commonly held jobs as barmaids in Australia. Women as barmaids participated in the dissemination of European culture, while at the same time staking out an economic place for themselves in the burgeoning alcohol trade.

Regulation of alcohol in Australia became a necessity. In colonial Australia men drank heavily, especially in pubs. These colonists not only drank beer but also spirits, especially rum. As a result, the government as well as social reformers moved to regulate drinking to a greater degree. For example, in 1816, the governor regulated the sale of manufactured beer and spirits. In a move to add more respectability to pubs the government passed a law in 1830 that mandated that pubs also had to be inns, complete with at least two rooms for rent. Pubs became known as both drinking and lodging establishments. In addition to governmental laws, the regulation of alcohol consumption took the form of temperance organizations, of which Australia saw a rise of during the late nineteenth-century. Some authors have argued that the increased immigration of women into Australia and the growth of family life led to a proliferation of these temperance movements. The abuse of spirits was the primary focus of these movements. As a way to curb drunkenness on spirits, breweries were established that brewed beer ostensibly for the health of the colonists. The development of a brewing industry did slowly change drinking habits from spirits to beer, which pleased temperance advocates. In addition to the move from spirits to beer, other ways to curb drinking developed. New forms of entertainment such as sports arose as popular leisure pastimes. Pubs and the masculinity they represented, however, remained the hallmarks of Australian society.

Pubs in colonial Australia were very much bastions of white male culture. Social and governmental regulations supported this fact. Even though most pubs had barmaids, women were shunned from drinking there. If women did drink in pubs men considered them to be "loose". Aboriginal men were also excluded from pubs. Beginning in 1838 the government passed laws that forbade aboriginal presence in and around licensed pubs. Aboriginal men could not obtain alcohol unless it was through the patronage of a white man. The exclusion of aboriginal men denigrated aboriginal manhood to such a great degree because drinking in pubs with other men was a sign of masculinity within Australian culture. Moreover, pubs were centers of power where men discussed politics and business, and thus women and aboriginal men were excluded from these important male power centers.

Australian independence did not bring an end to racist and sexist policies regarding alcohol. Aboriginals and women were still excluded from pubs. Australia's move to commonwealth status came to mean that drinking in pubs not only symbolized manhood and power but also citizenship. Some authors argue that by being excluded from pubs aboriginals and women were disenfranchised and denied a national identity. Eventually, between 1957 and

1975 the states finally accorded aboriginals the right to drink in public venues, and it began to be more common for women to drink in pubs in the later twentieth-century. Access to alcohol was such an important symbol of citizenship to aboriginals and women that as Ann McGrath wrote in her article "'Beneath the Skin': Australian Citizenship, Rights and Aboriginal Women," "The coming of alcohol was perceived by the majority of women and men as the most significant event of their recent times." In other words, more important even than the vote was the ability to drink alcohol publicly. Control over one's own access to it symbolized power, citizenship, and a move toward equality.

Conclusion

Comparisons of the production, trade, consumption, and regulation of alcohol among Africa, India, and Australia shed light on the continuities in European colonialism as well as the cultural distinctions across civilizations. Production and trade of alcohol in all three areas changed with colonization in several ways. First, all three regions began large-scale manufacturing of Western beer, attracting drinkers who wanted to identify with the West, both by drinking Western beer instead of indigenous beer, and by drinking as Westerners did, for leisure in pubs. Second, trade in alcohol became a very significant part of the colonial economy in all three areas. Both international and internal trade in alcohol skyrocketed during colonization as demand from African indigenous mine workers, Westernized Indians, and colonists in all three regions seemed insatiable. This demand allowed indigenous female beer makers in Africa a route to economic independence, dramatically changing indigenous gender roles. In India, the monopoly of the industry by the British colonial government enhanced demand by strongly linking alcohol with the British culture so sought after ambitious Indians. In Australia, the widespread proliferation of pubs in the colony demonstrated the high demand for alcohol as well as alcohol-based leisure, both of which became a defining characteristic of the colony and then the country. Moreover, these fast-multiplying pubs hired respectable young women to be barmaids, broadening the definition of femininity and allowing women a way to gain economic independence.

Consumption patterns in all three areas changed dramatically with colonization as well. First, one's alcohol preference came to define them in colonial society. In Africa young men who moved into the cash economy began to drink manufactured beer instead of indigenous beer, as they strove to be identified as urban, modern, and middle class. In India the British, along with the newly rich, educated, and Westernized Indians publicly displayed their status through their conspicuous consumption of Western alcohol. In Australia British colonial elites took pleasure in wine, which they believed demonstrated their refined culture as separate from that of the beer and spirits drinking masses. Furthermore, the white male population in Australia maintained a sense of exclusivity and privilege through excluding aborigines and women from their pubs. In all three instances alcohol consumption helped to solidify a distinction among classes. Second, drinking alcohol in pubs for leisure and entertainment brought a Western idea of leisure to the colonies. Third, the privilege of legally and rather freely drinking alcohol to socialize in public became an identifying characteristic of masculinity, allowing white men alone the ability to be masculine in Africa and Australia.

Regulation of alcohol provided more than one way to further the colonial project in all three areas. First, in the guise of keeping public order, regulation of alcohol by the colonial governments reinforced racism in Africa, India, and Australia. In South Africa the beerhall system that segregated black South Africans and rigidly regulated their drinking symbolized the oppression of the colonial and then apartheid governments. In India prohibitively high excise taxes on alcohol were meant to control drinking by the lower-classes. And in Australia the government outrightly outlawed drinking by aboriginals. In all three cases alcohol policies furthered racist agendas and came to symbolize the kind of ubiquitous oppression of colonism.

Second, in both Africa and India alcohol was in such high demand that the governments came to depend on its taxes each year. In Africa and India taxing alcohol was so lucrative that governments had little desire to promote temperance. Third, in Africa and India nationalist movements focused on self-determination over alcohol as a symbol of independence. Native Africans struggled for the rights to produce and drink alcohol where and when they pleased. In contrast, the independence movement in India wanted to prohibit alcohol as a repudiation of the Western culture that accompanied colonialism. In all of these ways, alcohol production, trade, consumption, and regulation shaped both the development and meanings of colonialism in the eighteenth and nineteenth-centuries in Africa, India, and Australia.

Further reading

Ambler, C. H. 1987. *Alcohol and Disorder in Pre-Colonial Africa.* Working Papers in African Studies No. 126. African Studies Center. Boston, MA: Boston University.
Bledsoe, C. and G. Pison. (eds.) 1994. *Nuptiality in Sub-Saharan Africa: Contemporary Anthropological and Demographic Perspectives.* Oxford: Clarendon Press.
Bowen, H. V., M. Lincoln, and N. Rigby. 2002. *The Worlds of the East India Company.* Rochester, NY: The Boydell Press.
Bryceson, D. F. (ed.) 2002. *Alcohol in Africa: Mixing Business, Pleasure, and Politics.* Portsmouth, NH: Heinemann.
Carlson, R. G. 1990. "Banana Beer, Reciprocity, and Ancestor Propitiation Among the Haya of Bukoba, Tanzania." *Ethnology.* 29 (4): 297–311.
Colson, E. and T. Scudder. 1988. *For Prayer and Profit: The Ritual, Economic, and Social Importance of Beer in Gwembe District, Zambia, 1950–1982.* Standford, CA: Stanford University Press.
Crush, J. and C. Ambler (eds.) 1992. *Liquor and Labor in Southern Africa.* Athens: Ohio University Press.

Heath, D. B. (ed.) 1995. *International Handbook on Alcohol and Culture.* Westport, CT: Greenwood Press.

Kirkby, D. 1997. *Barmaids: A History of Women's Work In Pubs.* Cambridge: Cambridge University Press.

La Hausse, P. 1988. *Brewers, Beerhalls and Boycotts: A History of Liquor in South Africa.* History Workshop Booklet. Johannesburg: Ravan.

McAllister, P. 2001. *Building the Homestead: Agriculture, Labour and Beer in South Africa's Transkei.* Leiden: Ashgate Publishing.

McGrath, A. 1993. "'Beneath the Skin': Australian Citizenship, Rights and Aboriginal Women" in R. Howe (ed.) "Women and the State", *Journal of Australian Studies.* 37 (June): 99–114.

Pan, L. 1975. *Alcohol in Colonial Africa.* Uppsala: The Scandinavian Institute of African Studies, and Helsinki: The Finnish Foundation for Alcohol Studies: 22.

Steinkraus, K. H. 1979. *Fermented Food Beverages in Nutrition.* Ed. C. Gastineau, W. J. Darby, and T. B. Turner. New York: Academic Press.

Wolcott, H. F. 1974. *The African Beer Gardens of Bulawayo: Integrated Drinking in a Segregated Society.* New Brunswick, NJ: Rutgers Center of Alcohol Studies.

7 Alcohol and globalization, Westernization, and tradition in the twentieth- and twentiety-first-centuries

Toward the end of the twentieth-century globalization transformed the world as post-Cold War contacts among the world's civilizations intensified. Trade, technology, and culture crossed political boundaries with ease. Global cultural transference was perhaps the most insidious aspect of globalization. The flood of culture across the globe was not only made up of Western culture, although that trend still predominated by the turn of the twenty-first-century, but increasingly non-Western cultures as well. Yet nowhere was globalization more readily apparent than in the arena of alcohol. Alcohol became a popular commodity in world trade, effectively spreading both Western and non-Western cultures across the world.

Global advertising promoted the spread of various kinds of alcohols across the globe. For example, because of advertising the world demanded tequila from Mexico, vodka from Russia, rum from the Caribbean, and whiskey from the United States. Wine especially was traded globally through international advertising, and its growing popularity led to its production in many parts of the world away from the most well known center of viticulture, Europe. "New World wines" came from the United States as well as parts of Canada, Australia, New Zealand, South America, and South Africa, to name a few. By 2001 New World wines had seized 35 percent of the global market away from Europe, whereas just 23 years earlier Europe had commanded 91 percent of the world wine trade. These changes in the wine trade represented just one aspect in the globalization of a much larger alcohol trade (from Kym Anderson in *The World's Wine Markets: Globalization at Work*).

Increases in production as well as domestic and international sales of alcohol attempted to meet its growing demand across the world. From the Second World War through the early twenty-first-century global alcohol consumption increased exponentially, especially in developed countries where people had more disposable income. According to Patrick E. McGovern in *Uncorking the Past: the Quest for Wine, Beer, and Other Alcoholic Beverages*, by the early twenty-first-century over "150 billion liters of beer, 27 billion liters of wine, and 2 billion liters of distilled spirits (mainly vodka) were produced worldwide." Alcohol was produced not only for international trade among developed countries, but also for trade to developing countries. Alcohol advertising crossed international boundaries resulting in the introduction of new kinds of alcohols globally. Convenient shipping as well as the ability to produce alcohol in many countries made the prices of alcohol affordable for many consumers across the world.

As consumption levels rose, virtually every society suffered from problems with alcohol abuse. Not only did abuse seriously weaken public health and safety in many countries, but mortality rates also increased, along with increases in liver, heart, and other chronic diseases, including HIV (if one links alcohol to increased dangerous sexual practices). One of the most insidious outcomes of the increase in use and abuse of alcohol, however, was violence. Sociologists argued that several factors led to such violence. One of the most important was the "pharmacological effects of alcohol." Some people, particularly men, when under the influence of alcohol behaved in the following ways: they took more risks, focused on the present instead of the possible results of their behavior, became hyperemotional, suffered from impaired judgment, and inflated their sense of male power. More men than women became violent; younger men rather than older men became violent; and socially or economically marginalized groups were more likely to become violent.

The proliferation of drinking establishments, which reflected as well as fostered the rapidly universalizing consumer culture, led to increased levels of acceptable violence as well. For example, in and around drinking establishments more violence was accepted than in other public venues. "Skid row" bars along with packed clubs fostered more violence, and employees that allowed higher levels of intoxication in effect promoted higher levels violence. Moreover, sexual competition, illegal activities, and "rowdy" music, along with lack of availability of food in the establishments led to more violent behavior. One study of Sydney, Australia showed that 44 percent of assaults and 60 percent of alcohol-related violence (not including domestic violence) occurred around licensed drinking establishments.

The transition of drinking establishments from cottage industries, where the bar owner knew the patrons and had more control over their behavior, to a kind of "night-time economy" based on impersonal control of the environment resulted in higher rates of violence as well. Kathryn Graham and Ross Homel in *Raising the Bar: Preventing Aggression in and Around Bars, Pubs and Clubs* argue that the renovation of run-down areas into large night clubs led to a focus on alcohol-based entertainment in many urban areas. Moreover, young adults under the influence of alcohol, thrown together in these highly sexualized environments brought about higher levels of aggression. The tremendous revenues earned by the clubs, along with the tax revenues gained by governments, contributed to the lax attitudes toward violence that accompanied such establishments. Laws against violence in and around drinking establishments existed, but were routinely ignored. In fact, the kinds of remedies for such socially destructive behavior tended to be directed at individuals. For example, establishments barred individual customers rather than solving the systemic link between alcohol and violence. Violence problems notwithstanding, alcohol grew as a global commodity in the twentieth- and twenty-first-centuries, spreading Western as well as non-Western cultures throughout the world.

Latin America

Worldwide sales of Mexican and Brazilian alcohol in the twentieth-century popularized Latin American culture globally. The growing international demand for culturally specific liquors compelled both Mexico and Brazil to argue for the exclusive rights over the alcohols identified with their countries, thus redefining the meaning of international intellectual property rights. Within Latin America, ceremonial use of traditional alcohols provided indigenous groups with a concrete means to maintain their culture in the face of modernization. Alcohol also shaped masculinity throughout Latin America; society expected that part of manhood included drinking more often and in higher quantities than women. Further shaping male identity, society equated male drunkenness with domestic violence, a widespread and under-documented public safety problem. In these several tangible ways alcohol perpetuated national, ethnic, and gender identities in Latin America.

Brazilian and Mexican alcohols provide examples of globalizing trends in alcohol sales. Brazilian cachaça, a distilled alcohol made from milled sugarcane, and first produced by and for slaves in Brazil in the sixteenth-century, became very popular worldwide toward the end of the twentieth-century. Because it was traditionally very cheap throughout much of the twentieth-century, Brazil's elites dismissed cachaça as a drink of poor Brazilians. During most of the twentieth-century it continued to be made mainly by small producers, but by the end of the twentieth-century large producers entered the market when cachaça became the main ingredient in a mixed drink called a caipirinha. The caipirinha became very trendy in high-class nightclubs in places like Paris and New York. In fact, in the early twenty-first-century cachaça was the second highest selling alcoholic beverage in Germany, just behind beer. And because of aggressive marketing by the Brazilian government it became a favorite drink among Brazil's elite as well.

Its popularity induced many other sugar-producing countries to make cachaça for an international market. As a result, Brazil petitioned the WTO (World Trade Organization) under the Trade Related Intellectual Property Rights agreement (TRIPS) to be the sole producer of cachaça. The Brazilian government hoped that the caipirinha would become Brazil's signature drink – much like the margarita was for Mexico and the mohito was for Cuba. Brazil did not want other countries cashing in on what it saw as a native product.

Like cachaça in Brazil, tequila in Mexico was in the forefront of twenty-first-century global trading trends. Over the twentieth-century it had become a very important export for Mexico. In 1999 alone the United States consumed 80 million liters of tequila. Moreover, Mexico made sure that NAFTA (North American Free Trade Agreement) stated that Mexico alone had the right to make tequila under the intellectual property rights law. The designation of cachaça and tequila as intellectual property became important commodities in international trade agreements, not only influenced how alcohol was traded, but also set a precedent for other kinds of intellectual property to be acknowledged.

World trade in alcohol, however, did not erase traditional forms of alcohol consumption in Latin America. For example, mezcal, a distilled version of the agave based, indigenous alcohol pulque, was still used in traditional ways by late twentieth-century Zapotec Indians living in the state of Oaxaca in Mexico. Zapotecs believed that mezcal should only be used ritually, and the villagers looked down upon excessive use of it outside of festivals and ceremonies. These ritualized drinking patterns date back to pre-colonial Mexico. In addition to the ritualized use of mezcal, the fermented drink, pulque, remained important in the diets of many rural and lower-class Mexicans. It contained thiamine, niacin, riboflavin, pantothenic acid, pyridoxine, vitamin B, and biotin. Per capita consumption of pulque in the late twentieth-century equaled about one liter per day, and even children drank pulque as part of their daily diet. Continuing to drink alcohol in traditional ways helped indigenous Mexicans hold on to their culture in spite of Westernization.

Even though cultural ideology dictated ceremonial use of alcohol for indigenous Mexicans, abuse existed throughout Mexico. In the late twentieth- and early twenty-first-centuries a large percentage of domestic violence cases were linked to alcohol abuse. Other kinds of violence, particularly in and around drinking establishments, brought alcohol abuse to the forefront of the Mexican government's health and safety concerns. The government began to require companies to put warning labels on bottles of alcohol. It also instituted a legal drinking age of 18. By the late twentieth-century Mexico also had a National Council on Addiction, which coordinated efforts to reduce problems with alcoholism. Regulations did not catch up with the problem, however, as alcohol continued to permeate people's lives in Latin America.

Africa

Alcohol in Africa shaped many of the same economic, social, and cultural structures as it did in Latin America. African countries struggled with the infiltration of Western culture and used alcohol in traditional ceremonies to maintain African identity. Moreover, non-cash trade, or gifting of indigenous alcohol continued to structure community hierarchies, and women's exclusive right to produce it shaped beliefs about gender. Women's separate income from their very profitable cottage alcohol industry gave them cash to buy imported goods, entering them into the global consumer society. As domestic alcohol industries modernized and Western alcohol imports grew, conspicuous consumption of these new alcohols provided middle- and upper-class Africans who wished to be modern, urban, and Western a way to display their identity. At the same time, conspicuous abstention provided Muslims and

Protestants with one of the most concrete ways to publicly demonstrate their identity in Africa.

Africa differed from Latin America in its experience with the international trade of alcohol, however. African alcohols were less successful on the international market, and production, trade, and consumption showed a pattern of continuity rather than change. In one example in Burkina Faso women in a cottage industry setting continued to produce red sorghum beer in a customary way well into the twenty-first-century. Beer production remained strictly gender specific. The art of beermaking generally was passed down matrilineally; some female brewers came from a long line of brewers – mothers, grandmothers, and great grandmothers. In these cases a woman might receive help from her female relatives to start or maintain her business.

Producing red sorghum beer was labor intensive and it took three days and at least three women. The women boiled the ingredients the first day for four hours and the second day for eight to nine hours. By the third day the beer was ready to sell to women marketers who then sold it to small taverns or other outlets for resell. These beermakers created networks with the women who marketed the beer to taverns. Not all transactions were cash transactions, however. During the processing of the beer, women often gave some of it away to those who helped make it as payment in kind. Friends and neighbors usually received free beer before the brewer sold it to others. Moreover, a tradition called "lenga" existed, which granted the buyer of the beer a taste before buying it. Elites received a larger "taste" and finally the chief received an entire calabash of beer before he had to buy. In addition to making beer to sell, women in small towns still made red sorghum beer for many ritual and ceremonial occasions. Villagers consumed red sorghum beer for work parties and ceremonies. One of the most important occasions was the memorial festival commemorating one's dead ancestors, which happened several years after the death of the relative. The village always commissioned women to make beer for these celebrations, which were very expensive and elaborate.

While women produced the beer almost exclusively, men grew much of the grain. Early in the second half of the twentieth-century married couples still had separate budgets so a woman could buy grain or malt from her husband and then sell him the beer after she made it, making a profit for herself. Women used some of their profits from selling beer, which could be substantial, to buy imported manufactured items. So even though beermaking and selling remained traditional, its profits brought these women into the international market through their purchases.

Westernization infiltrated Burkina Faso through Catholic missionaries, causing conversion to Catholicism to increase in the late twentieth-century. This cultural change complicated the economic situation for female beer makers. Catholic couples now had joint accounts, rather than the usual separate accounts held before their conversion to Catholicism. In these cases the husband might invest in the business of the brewing wife in order to make more money for the entire family. This new kind of arrangement frequently ended up being disadvantageous for the woman because she no longer sold her product to her husband, and the profits no longer went to her, but to the family unit where the husband held greater power. Moreover, as a result of modernization, women began to be usurped by large producers. Many women ended up merely selling the beer for the large producers rather than making beer for their own small enterprise, taking away much of their economic independence. The move away from cottage industry to large producers also signified the modernization of a significant piece of traditional culture.

Modernization and global trends not only brought changes in production and trade, but also brought changes in consumption of alcohol as well. The global trend of high alcohol consumption in the second half of the twentieth-century held true in Burkina Faso also. In 1970 over 700 million liters of traditional beer was consumed. Traditional beer continued to be an extremely important commodity in the local economies. Change took place in the late twentieth-century, however, because many of the people in Burkina Faso became either Catholic or Muslim. So by the early part of the twenty-first century in the Muslim areas very little alcohol consumption took place. In the Catholic areas people still used alcohol, but for Catholic ceremonies such as name day commemorations rather than for traditional rituals. In this way the change in alcohol consumption habits, brought on by the global spread of religions, signaled a move away from traditional, African culture.

In Burkina Faso an increase in the consumption of Western-style beer transformed the beer market, which had been formerly controlled solely by indigenous beer. Bottled beer became popular in the larger towns where refrigeration was available. In addition, in market towns richer farmers began to drink bottled beer instead of sorghum beer when they brought their goods to market. By the end of the twentieth-century drinking it became a status symbol for the urban elite who could afford to drink the more expensive bottled beer. Westernization in the twentieth- and early twenty-first-centuries made its way into African towns through manufactured beer. Bottled beer consumption further signified one's place in the middle- and upper-classes in Burkina Faso.

Consumption habits in another part of Africa, Zambia, reflected Westernization as well. For example, in the late twentieth-century over 50 percent of Zambians abstained, which could partially be explained by a rise in Protestantism, a Western religion. Just under 15 percent of the population still claimed to be heavy drinkers, however. These heavy drinkers drank two to three times a week and drank to inebriation. Most heavy drinkers were married men over 30 with varied educational and economic status. Since the heavy drinkers were primarily men, alcohol consumption patterns furthered gender differences, but drinking patterns did not seem to further class differences because male heavy drinkers came from all classes and educational levels.

Alcohol consumption habits of rural and urban dwellers in Zambia differed. Rural dwellers more often drank homemade beer. In the city, though, national advertising of manufactured beer influenced the consumption patterns of the urban elite. Elite urbanites almost exclusively drank bottled beer, publicly demonstrating their higher place in the social hierarchy. Moreover, sometimes elites drank international alcohol products and thus were pulled into a globalizing culture through their alcohol choices.

Unfortunately, consumption of alcohol by Zambian men of all classes perpetuated the spread of HIV/AIDS in the late twentieth- and early twenty-first-centuries in that country. Since many men drank in bars without their wives, and reported having sex with women other than their regular partners, there was a strong correlation between the spread of HIV/AIDS and alcohol. As a result of unprotected, alcohol-included male philandering, many women and children contracted a disease that ravaged the country. By the early twenty-first-century, 18 percent of Zambian women were HIV positive. Moreover, many STDs were passed along in the same way. Of those who drank at least once a week, 37 percent had STDs, while of those who did not drink, 23 percent had STDs. Little or no alcohol regulation addressed the problem of the spread of STDs. The meager regulation of drinking in Zambia took the form of employee assistance programs to help staff with alcohol-related problems. The best assurance of abstinence, however, seemed to be participation in Protestantism or Islam, since one's drinking habits overtly signified his or her identity in African society.

Saudi Arabia

In Saudi Arabia the strict ban on alcohol production, consumption, and regulation symbolized the culture's complete adherence to Islam. The rise in illegal production and trade, as well as the increase in consumption in the late twentieth and early twenty-first-centuries, then, represented a small yet noticeable infiltration of Western values and global consumer culture. As abuse rose during the same time period, Western ideology spread, too, as Saudi leaders reluctantly adopted a Western-style treatment protocol and began to define alcohol abuse as a disease, rather than as a failure to adhere to Islam.

Production and trade of alcohol was against the law in Saudi Arabia in the twentieth-century and remained so in the early twenty-first-century. Alcohol traders, however, continued to smuggle it into the eastern part of the country from Bahrain or Jordan where alcohol was available. For example, the Saudi Customs Department reported that it confiscated 88,000 bottles of alcohol in 2010 (Asa Trulsson, "Drugs, Alcohol and Holy Denial," http://www.utrikesper spektiv.se/2011/06/10/stat-och-samhalle/drugs-alcohol-and-holy-denial/, accessed December 14, 2011). Entrepreneurs and individual households also illegally produced many kinds of homemade alcohol, including fermented grapes or dates and a distilled 190 proof spirit called sadiqii.

The unlawful production and trade of alcohol supplied a growing demand in the late twentieth-century. Researchers argued that alcohol consumption began to rise at that time for a number of reasons, all stemming from the tremendous oil wealth that started flowing into Saudi Arabia in the 1970s and 1980s. For example, oil wealth made international travel possible for Saudi elites, who brought back Westernized views of alcohol. Moreover, increased alcohol consumption followed the arrival of the internet, Western movies, global television broadcasting, and the large number of foreign workers who appeared in Saudi Arabia since the 1980s, as signs of Westernization grew. Furthermore, the rapid population growth after the 1970s resulted in a young population who were more influenced by Western culture. In fact, people who had some knowledge of alcohol garnered a certain degree of social capital in personal circles in Saudi society in the late twentieth- and early twenty-first-centuries.

In addition, anecdotal evidence uncovered alcohol use in Western-styled social settings by privileged segments of society. WikiLeaks reported that alcohol could be found at elite parties, and American diplomats told stories of "private" nightclubs that not only served alcohol to both men and women, but also offered dancing to their patrons. Official Saudi consumption rates remained some of the lowest in the world, however, at between 0.25 and 0.6 liters per capita, depending on the source. Drinking also remained such a stigma in the general population that a woman could apply for divorce if her husband drank, and fathers had the right to prohibit their daughters from marrying a man whose father was a known drinker.

The most concrete evidence for rising "unofficial" alcohol consumption arose from statistics on increasing abuse problems. While most Saudi citizens still believed that practicing Islam was the best solution to the problem of alcohol abuse, the Saudi government was forced to provide social services to address the growing problem in the late 1980s. They opened three drug and alcohol treatment hospitals and blanketed the country with a media campaign against drug and alcohol use and abuse. Yet the problem persisted.

By 2003 the WHO (World Health Organization) reported that 24 percent of the patients in one substance abuse hospital had used alcohol and 12 percent had abused alcohol. Virtually all patients in these hospitals were young men, with women constituting only 0.02 percent of the residents. These men, whose average age was 29, cited peer pressure or unemployment as the reason for their addiction. As these statistics on alcoholism came to light, researchers began to examine the social ramifications of alcoholism. For example, a 2006 study on Saudi Arabia correlated alcohol abuse and domestic violence. The study also argued that the continued social stigma around alcohol "exacerbated the effects of alcohol (ab)use within families." (In Abdulaziz A. Albrithen, "Alcoholism and Domestic Violence in Saudi Society.") In addition, because the Saudi government did not officially recognize domestic violence, the problem remained difficult to address.

By the end of the first decade of the twenty-first-century the continued rapid urbanization, modernization, and industrialization had exacerbated alcohol abuse. A 2009 survey of medical students in Riyadh revealed that 75 percent of them believed substance abuse was a problem among young men ages 15 to 30. Furthermore, increased abuse problems made the international news in 2010 when a prominent, UK-educated Saudi doctor and researcher traveled to Detroit, an area with a large Arab-American and Muslim population, to tour one of the oldest alcohol treatment centers in the United States. He sought advice from the directors because he, along with other prominent Saudi healthcare experts, planned to open a 250-bed alcohol and drug treatment hospital in their country. He also had plans to open several more hospitals throughout Saudi Arabia to address the growing addiction problem across the Islamic Middle East. This Western-educated doctor also believed that a 12-step program, modeled after AA, but tailored to an Islamic population, should follow hospitalization.

Even though treatment became available, the government still relied on strict regulation to deter not only alcohol abuse, but also any association with alcohol at all. Even into the twenty-first-century Saudi Arabia maintained the most conservative alcohol laws in the Islamic Middle East. Alcohol policies had always been stringent under the leadership of the Saud dynasty, members of a conservative subgroup of Sunni Islam that believed in a very rigid interpretation of the Quran. Therefore, Saudi law was based on Islam, and the government employed "Islamic police" to rigorously enforce Islamic values. For example, alcohol production or sale resulted in lashings, imprisonment, or even execution. Yet even with these deterrents the production, trade, use, and abuse of alcohol rose in Saudi Arabia in the late twentieth-century. Between 1983 and 2002 alcohol infractions increased by over 300 percent.

After the turn of the twenty-first-century the government seemed to turn its focus from personal use to the production and sale of alcohol. The government now legally ensured treatment for substance abuse sufferers at rehabilitation hospitals, and in 2004, while it blocked the majority of pornography and drug sites on the web, it only blocked one alcohol site out of 60,000. Conversely, it stiffened the penalties for smuggling or selling alcohol, resulting in larger fines, more lashings, longer prison sentences, and higher frequencies of the death penalty. The looser restrictions on personal consumption, however, and the growth of Western-style treatment facilities revealed the government's subtle recognition of a penetration of Western values.

India

As India developed in the later twentieth-century, it began mass production of both Western and indigenous alcohols. Demand for Western alcohol grew as it became a symbol of cultural Westernization. At the same time, many Indians still drank indigenous alcohol, publically demonstrating their desire to preserve Indian culture. Nevertheless, Indian consumption of all alcohols, including indigenous, illegal, and Western jumped in the twentieth-century, indicating India's participation in a global consumer culture as wealth grew in that country. Increased consumption, however, led to increased abuse, which brought on serious public health and safety problems. In response, Western-style Alcoholics Anonymous groups emerged, ushering in yet another Western cultural construct, the disease model of alcohol abuse. Yet the highly contradictory roles of alcohol still plagued India's government, because like many other governments around the world, it wrestled with curbing public over-consumption and its consequences, while at the same time heavily relying on alcohol taxes.

By the late twentieth-century three major kinds of liquor existed in India. First, many Indians still produced indigenous liquor. One of these, called arrack, was distilled from grains, rice, and sugarcane. In addition to arrack, Indians produced several kinds of indigenous palm wine. Both arrack and palm wine remained popular up through the early twenty-first-century. Second, Indians produced a substantial amount of illicit or bootleg liquor. Exactly how much was still unknown by the early twenty-first-century, but it was clear that illegal alcohol production was prevalent. Third, Indians produced "Indian-made foreign liquor," which included Western kinds of liquor such as beer and distilled spirits like whiskey, gin, brandy, and rum. The production of these Western liquors rose by 12 to 15 percent in the 1990s. The popularity of foreign liquor in general, from many areas of the world, brought a global culture to the doorstep of the elite and middle-class Indians who could afford to purchase it.

All classes in India increased their alcohol consumption in the late twentieth- and early twenty-first-centuries. The integration of India into global markets in the latter part of the twentieth-century helped to bring about this change. Many researchers argue that global alcohol advertising urged middle-class Indians, especially, to become less conservative and to take on modern, perhaps more Western values by drinking more liquor. In addition, marketing and mass production of alcohol, and thus its increased availability influenced the rural poor to increase their consumption as well. The poor, however, still had fewer means and thus could not afford the expensive, foreign alcohol. Drinking alcohol, especially Western alcohol, by the elite and middle-classes became even more of a status symbol in the early twenty-first-century. Drinking turned out to be a visible way to set themselves apart from the lower-class.

Along with increased consumption of alcohol came abuse. Popular media at the end of the twentieth-century indicated that problems with excessive alcohol consumption were on the rise. For example, a study in one state found that over 20 percent of the population above the age of ten abused alcohol. Another indicator of increased alcohol problems came from the intake statistics of mental health hospitals. For example, between 1953 and 1965 no patients with alcohol problems were admitted, but by 1994, 25 percent of the patients admitted had alcohol problems. In addition, by the late twentieth-century drivers under the influence of alcohol caused an estimated 25 percent of road accidents.

Governmental regulation of alcohol in India during the late twentieth- and early twenty-first-centuries was checkered. While early twentieth-century independence movements championed prohibition legislation, these laws did not last. The negative tax consequences were too devastating for the states involved. Various states did experiment with prohibition, but by the late 1990s only one state remained dry. As a result, regulation of alcohol took the form of social rather than governmental control as Western-style Alcoholics Anonymous groups multiplied. At first these groups only operated in English, but there was such a demand that they opened chapters in local languages. The spreading culture of Alcoholics Anonymous ideology indicated a penetration of Western values throughout India. Western attitudes toward alcohol in general became emblematic of the Westernization of India in the twentieth- and twenty-first-centuries.

China

In China, the dramatic increases in production, trade, consumption, abuse, and regulation of alcohol in the late twentieth- and early twenty-first-centuries spearheaded cultural modernization and Westernization in that country. Chinese businessmen in particular publicly drank expensive alcohol to flaunt their success. Yet alcohol also helped the Chinese repel aspects of the West, as they continued to use alcohol in traditional social ceremonies and drink the indigenous alcohol baijiu. Chinese society also expected that men drank more than women and tacitly approved of male public drunkenness, illustrating how attitudes about alcohol shaped definitions of masculinity in that country. As alcohol abuse grew, civic responses to the problem took the form of a growing Alcoholics Anonymous movement. This movement ushered in yet another Western ideology, one that both defined alcohol abuse as a disease and used the US generated 12-step program to help.

China, like India, bought more foreign liquor and produced larger quantities of it by the late twentieth- and early twenty-first-centuries. Chinese trade in alcohol rose tremendously with China's move into the international economy. Because of the opening of international markets, the sale of foreign liquors to China doubled in the early 1990s. Not only did sales of foreign liquors rise, but also sales of domestic alcohol products, especially beer, rose as well. By the end of the century China was the second largest beer producer next to the United States. Moreover, the number of drinking establishments skyrocketed. Many scholars argue that advertising played an important role in the increase in Chinese liquor sales. Alcohol producers spent millions of dollars on advertising; by 1995 almost 20 percent of all television advertising was liquor related. Liquor had become a very popular commodity during the globalization of China's economy in the late twentieth-century.

Even though imported alcohol began to claim a larger part of the liquor market in China, many Chinese drinkers still preferred baijiu, a traditional liquor made from sorghum, rice, and unhusked barley. Moreover, the Chinese did not all become modern, Western-style leisure drinkers, rather many still used alcohol in ceremonial ways. For example, at the most important festival of the year, the Chinese New Year, also called the Spring Festival, an alcohol called tusu, which was made from peppers and cypress leaves, prevailed. It symbolized health, luck, and long life. Alcohol remained a central feature of many other rituals and celebrations as well. Alcohol continued to be important in wedding ceremonies for many ethnic groups in China. For example, in one practice the bridegroom's family offered alcohol to the bride's family, and when the bride's family drank the alcohol, it symbolized the solidification of the engagement. Also, during a marriage ceremony the bride and groom drank alcohol out of the same cup, and the groom toasted members of the bride's family and friends. In these ways many Chinese used alcohol to maintain their traditional culture even as China's economy became global.

China's growing economy, which brought on a jump in production and sale of alcohol, also ushered in a dramatic increase in consumption as well as a change in consumption patterns for many Chinese. Political developments also increased consumption. In 1976, with the news of the arrest of the "Gang of Four" at the end of the Cultural Revolution, wine shops quickly sold out of wine. Moreover, alcohol consumption rose by 100 percent between the end of the Cultural Revolution and 1995. A new elite, mainly merchants, began to drink more alcohol publicly, showing off their economic ability to consume. Many kinds of drinking games came into fashion. One such game required the participant to make up a specific kind of poem. If he (most drinkers were men) could not comply quickly, he was forced to take a drink. In addition to playing drinking games these new elites exhibited a high rate of public drunkenness, even though public drunkenness was traditionally looked down upon. Drinking and flouting social norms allowed them to show off their high status. Their relationship to alcohol set them apart from other segments of society, signifying their place in China's new elite class.

Increased alcohol consumption became a leading indicator of China's expanding economy. For example, in 2006 the Chinese made up 20 percent of the world's alcohol consumers. The Chinese also consumed the most spirits by volume, 3.6 billion liters per year. Spirits were very popular in China because their high alcohol content produced more intoxication for the money than did other alcohols. Another pattern surfaced as a result of China's economic growth; the rich Chinese not only drank more alcohol, but they also began to drink more expensive alcohol. These alcohol consumption patterns brought China into line with global cultural trends.

An alcohol abuse problem arose with the overall increase in alcohol consumption, however. More men than women drank and therefore problem drinkers tended to be men instead of women. Those in the middle-classes had fewer problems with alcohol than the elite or lower class. A study of 17 psychiatric hospitals revealed that between 1980 and 1993 the number of patients admitted with alcohol problems increased by 400 percent. By 1995 a whopping 50 percent of the traffic accidents were alcohol related. As a result, social remedies emerged. "Alcohol clubs," similar to Alcoholics Anonymous, were set up to alleviate the increasing problem of abuse. The government also reacted. In an attempt to regulate alcohol consumption the government instituted an alcohol tax. By the beginning of the twenty-first-century the tax was so high that in order to consume much alcohol one had to be relatively wealthy. This tax on alcohol did discourage lower-class drinking but it also furthered the separation of elite culture from that of the rest of society.

The increase in alcohol problems in the late twentieth-century did not mean that China had a high rate of alcoholism compared to other countries, however. By the first decade of the twenty-first-century it was still more common to drink alcohol slowly with meals or on ceremonial occasions. It continued to be common to drink with groups rather than to drink alone, which some authors argue led to less alcoholism. Moreover, a large number of Chinese did not drink at all. One explanation for lower levels of alcohol consumption, according to some researchers, was the flushing response experienced by Asians, which included a rise in body temperature, heart beat, perspiration, nausea, headache, and a flushing of the face when drinking alcohol, which made drinking alcohol less pleasurable. Other researchers argue against this explanation because other Asian cultures such as Japan had high rates of consumption. Even with relatively low consumption and abuse rates, China's new relationship to alcohol signaled its response to modernization and Westernization.

Japan

Skyrocketing alcohol consumption in Japan allowed the Japanese to show their enthusiastic adoption of Western culture, while at the same time alcohol also allowed them to preserve core Japanese values. There was aggressive marketing of not only Western alcohol, but also Western drinking habits, noticeably Westernized Japanese culture. Yet the choreographed ceremonial approach to drinking, even in modern settings, provided the Japanese with a way to overtly adhere to tradition. Moreover, Japan's government benefitted from the high demand through alcohol taxes that appreciably bolstered the national budget, demonstrating alcohol's importance not only to society but also to the political structure that held it together.

The alcohol trade in Japan increased rapidly in the latter part of the twentieth century. The industry modernized and alcohol producers turned to Western-style marketing strategies, which changed drinking culture. For example, by the late twentieth-century beer producers marketed so many varieties of beer that it became more common for drinkers to each order something different in a bar rather than to order one kind of alcohol as a group, as had been the tradition. Alcohol companies continued to strategize about ways to increase individual consumption, which they believed would lead to more drinking. Companies began to market shochu, a traditional, distilled drink, in individual cans in the 1980s. These individual cans became very popular because one company came out with cans of shochu mixed with fruit juice. In addition, sake and beer began to be marketed in single-sized packaging to promote individual choice. One beer company increased its sales of beer because it marketed individual beer cans as masculine. Moreover, alcohol became available in vending machines. Machines stayed open later than liquor stores and opened at 5 am. These trends in alcohol marketing furthered the Western cultural idea of individualism, and thus furthered Westernization.

Following world trends, alcohol consumption increased tremendously in Japan after the Second World War. Between 1950 and 1980 alcohol consumption increased by 800 percent. Some argue that it leveled off in the 1980s. Others argue, however, that it continued to increase through the first part of the twenty-first-century, rising by as much as 1,000 percent overall and 400 percent per capita. Drinking alcohol came to represent one's ability to spend disposable income on leisure activities. It thus became a visible way to separate the rising middle- and upper-classes from the lower-class.

Not only did consumption increase, but tastes in alcohol also began to change. Sake had been the traditional drink of choice, but beer overtook sake in popularity by the late twentieth-century. By the end of the twentieth-century the Japanese drank three times more beer than they did sake. In fact, between the Second World War and the beginning of the twenty-first-century beer drinking increased by 3,000 percent. Whiskey consumption also increased between the Second World War and the first decade of the twenty-first-century. Some argue that it increased as much as 5,500 percent and that by 2010 it made up 25 percent of Japan's alcohol consumption. Others contend, however, that it accounted for much less. Some researchers estimate that alcohol by preference in Japan in 2010 was 66 percent beer, 22 percent sake, 5 percent whiskey, and 4 percent shochu. In any case, as incomes rose and tariffs on whiskey decreased people did consume much more of it. Another new trend that emerged toward the end of the century had people ordering wine more often when they dined out. Moreover, more people drank at home or at sporting events than had traditionally been the case. The addition of new drinking venues as well as the increased consumption of beer, whiskey, and wine furthered the Westernization of culture in the lives of many Japanese.

Even though much drinking behavior changed in the late twentieth- and early twenty-first-centuries, many traditional consumption patterns remained. For example, at social gatherings for businessmen (it was mainly a male drinking culture) it was still common for the employee first to offer a drink, often sake, to his boss. The employee held the drink in two hands while offering it to his boss and the boss received it with one hand, signifying his superior position. After his superior drank, he would offer his employee a drink with one hand while the employee received it with two hands. This etiquette worked the same way when older and younger people drank together on social occasions. Moreover, traditionally at these social occasions one never served oneself, and it was acceptable for men to exhibit drunken behavior while in public. Therefore holding onto traditional drinking habits, even while participating in modern business transactions, was a way to hold onto traditional culture in the face of Westernization and modernization.

Syncretism of cultures existed as well. For example, many people began to drink whiskey, a Western alcohol, yet they ordered it as a group, strengthening traditional group culture. One member of the group would order a bottle of whiskey with enough glasses for everyone, and the whole group would drink the same thing. In this situation, people did not serve themselves either. A waitress or a woman in the group would serve the whiskey. These continuities in drinking patterns helped maintain Japanese culture as Japan's economy went global.

The tremendous increase in alcohol consumption also brought abuse, however. The number of alcoholics in Japan increased from 2 percent of the population after the Second World War to 6 percent in the late twentieth-century. The government continued to regulate alcohol by enforcing its legal drinking age of 20. It also taxed alcohol. In the 1990s alcohol taxes accounted for at least 3 percent of the national budget. There was not a rise of any sort of temperance movement, however, because heavy drinking had traditionally been an acceptable way to relax in Japan.

Russia

The state in Soviet Russia attempted to control all aspects of the production, sale, and consumption of alcohol during its time in power in the twentieth-century. Alcohol demand was already high at the beginning of the twentieth-century and it rose throughout, even though it was highly regulated. Alcohol became the primary coping mechanism during the years of scarcity of consumer and entertainment goods in Soviet Russia. Alcohol continued to dominate the lives of many in the 1990s and 2000s after the fall of the Soviet government. As the economy moved to a free market system, many Russians used alcohol to cope with the severe social and economic upheaval, while the new elite demonstrated their place in the global consumer society by their conspicuous consumption of expensive liquor. Alcohol in the free market also allowed Russia to penetrate the global demand for exotic alcohols after the turn of the twenty-first-century, through its trade in the distinctly Russian samogon, which spread an idealized Russian culture to the West.

During the Soviet years alcohol profits alone allowed the state to maintain fiscal solvency. After the end of Soviet state monopoly on alcohol in the 1990s, the crucial role that alcohol profits had played became glaringly apparent to the new, struggling government. Soviet and post-Soviet regulations on alcohol did not prevent serious problems with abuse, and an unsuccessful campaign against alcohol in the 1980s simply reinforced the centrality of alcohol to Russian society and cultural identity. The extremely high consumption rates of Russian men remained a defining aspect of Russian masculinity, while male alcohol abuse became the number one crisis in public health and safety, especially in the 1990s and beyond.

In the 1920s Stalin mandated a state monopoly on the commodity. He calculated that because of the propensity for Russians to drink, the substantial alcohol profits would be crucial to the solvency of the government. He was correct. In 1940 "there were more shops selling drink than meat, fruit and vegetables put together." (Stephen White in *Russia Goes Dry: Alcohol,*

State and Society.) At the same time, however, the USSR wanted to present a carefully orchestrated picture of life in Russia that did not include any social problems such as alcohol abuse. So by the 1960s the government chose to hide alcohol production rates by grouping them into one category together with ice cream, coffee, cocoa, mushrooms, and spices. Some estimates, however, indicated that legal production of spirits rose by 300 percent between 1940 and 1980, even with a phenomenal 262 percent price increase during the same period.

Price increases did not result from an increase in production costs, however. Instead they represented attempts by the Soviet government to curtail drinking, as well as to bolster the treasury. In fact, some estimates concluded that 92 percent of the purchase price of vodka went to the government, accounting for 13 to 14 percent of the entire state budget. In 1992, however, after the end of the Soviet era, the government abolished its monopoly on alcohol sales. The losses were so great to the financially strapped new government that the Duma attempted to bring back the state monopoly in 2006.

During the twentieth-century, however, legal alcohol accounted for only 60 to 70 percent of all the liquor sold in Russia. Homebrew, called samogon, made up the other 30 to 40 percent of the alcohol produced, bringing in profits to the brewers of as high as 800 percent. The risk to the brewer was great, though, because they could be sentenced to several years in jail if caught. After the fall of the Soviet Union, the new state moved toward legalizing homebrewing in 1992 in an attempt to adequately regulate all alcohol sales. It remained illegal for people to peddle samogon without a license, but in numerous rural villages brewers flouted these regulations. In fact, more people took up brewing and selling samogon. Its sales supported numerous people during the difficult economic times of the early 1990s. It even became a form of currency in some areas. Its price, about 55 percent of the price of vodka, made it even more popular. In 2003 a private company secured a license and began selling samogon legally. The company created its own brand, and even though its samogon sold for three to four times the price of vodka, in 2007 the turnover for the liquor reached five million dollars. This exclusively Russian brand became popular in Russia and by 2011 the company marketed it to the United States as an authentically Russian spirit, even more so than vodka. With the high demand for exotic alcohols in the West, samogon received a positive reception. It made a noticeable impact when a cocktail made from the spirit, called "From Russia with Love" won a prize at the prestigious Ultimate Beverage Challenge contest in 2011.

Alcohol fed an ever-growing consumer demand from the Russian populace over the twentieth- and early twenty-first-centuries. With the exception of the years 1985 to 1988 consumption of alcohol rose steadily. One study found that per capita alcohol consumption increased from 7.3 liters in 1955 to 15.2 liters in 1979. Another study came to a wildly different finding, asserting that the consumption of alcohol increased by an astounding 800 percent between 1940 and 1984. By the 1970s, Russia ranked eighth worldwide in the consumption of all alcohol, and fourth in the consumption of hard liquor. By some estimates, Russians spent between 15 and 20 percent of their disposable income on liquor. By the 1980s a surprising 90 percent of women, who traditionally had relatively low rates of consumption, drank regularly, which correlated with an increase in birth defects. Consumption also increased in other populations as well. By the 1980s almost 80 percent of high school students had tried alcohol. These statistics did not account for the rampant alcohol theft that consistently took place during the Soviet years.

In the new market economy of the early 1990s consumption rates continued to rise. A 30 percent increase occurred within just a few years, perhaps reflecting the social upheavals of the time. Not surprisingly then, by 1993 Russia surpassed France in per capita consumption of alcohol, "with an average consumption of a bottle of vodka for every adult male every two days." (Stephen White, *Russia Goes Dry: Alcohol, State and Society.*) Some companies even paid their workers in vodka because of the shortage of money in early post-Soviet Russia. By 2007, after over 15 years of a new government and economy, consumption rates remained high, at 15 liters per year. At that time the government increased efforts to decrease consumption, and by 2010 the levels dropped to 12.5 liters per year.

High consumption rates led to widespread abuse during the entire Soviet era and beyond. During the early years of the Soviet government, leaders considered alcoholism a hold over from Russia's bourgeois past. But that explanation ceased to hold any credence as abuse rates continually rose throughout the twentieth-century. Alcohol abuse skyrocketed during the 1970s and early 1980s. By the mid 1980s almost 15 percent of the population were alcoholics. Many believed the lack of available alternative entertainment, caused by a government that paid little attention to consumer goods and services, led to the rise.

The abuse spawned myriad social problems. One survey of 500 divorcees showed that almost 40 percent of the complainants cited drunkenness as the problem. In addition, alcohol led to over 30 percent of all auto accidents and 80 percent of all deaths resulting from auto accidents. According to court statistics people under the influence of alcohol committed roughly 74 percent of all murders, 70 percent of all rapes, and 50 percent of all robberies in Russia. Moreover, alcohol abuse caused a considerable decrease in manufacturing output because of absenteeism, especially on Mondays. Workers lost up to 40 days a year of production time because of alcohol abuse. Abuse was so prevalent that during the 1983 Soviet Central Committee meeting it was finally recognized as a serious social problem. When Gorbachev came to power and the government gradually opened up, Alcoholics Anonymous was allowed to start groups within the country. And churches, which were given more rights in post-Soviet Russia, also vocally promoted sobriety.

The post-Soviet collapse of the economy in the 1990s caused an escalation in alcohol abuse and its attendant social problems. By some estimates 30 percent of the population suffered from alcohol problems by 1993. The number of crimes committed while drunk rose, and because, like the rest of the population, 30 percent of the police force abused alcohol, enforcement of the laws deteriorated. Alcohol abuse so deeply permeated society that a marked increase in mortality rates occurred between 1980 and 1994. Life expectancy for men fell from 61 to 57. To address the substantial increase in alcohol abuse in the 1990s, sobriety movements advocated for legislation regulating drinking, but the majority of the public did not support these movements.

Serious social problems continued into the twenty-first-century. In 2002 the WHO (World Health Organization) estimated that 18 percent of Russian men between the ages of 20 and 64 died from alcohol-related problems. By 2005 some studies showed that alcohol-related male mortality rates had risen to 31 percent for those between the ages of 20 and 44. For women of the same age alcohol-related mortality was smaller, yet still a sizeable 20 percent of all deaths. Between 2007 and 2011 most statistics reported male life expectancy to be 60—higher than the age of 57 reported in 1994—yet still resulting in one of the lowest life expectancies in Europe, compared to Germany, for example, where male life expectancy was 77 in 2009. Russian women, however, who had much lower abuse rates than men, lived an average of 73 years. In yet another bleak study it was reported that while 18-year-old men in the West had "a ninety percent chance of reaching retirement age ... for young men in Russia the odds are reduced to fifty percent." (Grace Wong, "Russia's Bleak Picture of Health.") These findings caused Russian leaders Vladamir Putin and Dmitry Medvedev to proclaim alcoholism a national security threat in 2011.

The serious alcohol abuse problems also led to a frightening number of alcohol poisonings across Russia. In 2006 over 40,000 people died from alcohol poisoning, compared to 300 in the much more populated United States. The consumption of alternative forms of alcohol, such as cologne, window cleaner, antifreeze, and de-icing fluids, to name a few, led to many of these deaths. Consumption of non-beverage alcohol rose to such crisis proportions that in 2006 the government instituted laws regulating the use of these substances. High rates of alcohol poisoning also came from the Russian habit of binge drinking. There is even a specific word in Russian, *zapoi*, which means "a continuous state of drunkenness over a period of two or more days where the person does not engage in normal social life." By 2008 the number of deaths attributed to alcohol poisoning had dropped to 19,000 because of the efforts of the government to regulate alcohol.

Problems with the regulation of alcohol plagued the Soviet government throughout the twentieth-century. Early on the Bolshevik government attempted prohibition, but it soon failed. So in the 1920s the government resorted to establishing commissions for the treatment of alcoholism. The party also sponsored Anti-Alcohol Societies, to which over 250,000 people belonged by 1929. By the early 1930s, though, the government eliminated a focus on alcoholism and instead concentrated on better living standards for the working class. They did, however, continue to require many abusers to go to rehabilitation centers, several of which resembled prisons.

Finally, toward the end of the Soviet era, the government under Mikhail Gorbachev, himself urged on by his wife and at least two of his close advisors, began a concerted campaign against alcoholism. Starting in 1985 the government formed a temperance society, the state-controlled media published extensive anti-alcohol propaganda, and several governmental and party organizations promoted the campaign. The program included outlawing alcohol at all governmental gatherings, raising the legal drinking age to 21, and increasing fines and penalties for alcohol-related disorderly conduct. Moreover, the government eliminated hundreds of alcohol outlets and increased the price of vodka by so much that it took 19 hours of an average worker's wages to buy a bottle. In addition, the government attempted to eliminate homebrewing. Penalties for the possession of homebrew equipment included up to two years of hard labor and a substantial fine.

The 1985 regulations did bring about change. Crime decreased and public health improved. For example, mortality rates for men dropped considerably. People continued to demand alcohol, however. Customers waiting in lines outside the limited number of alcohol shops numbered in the hundreds in some urban areas, causing Moscow, for example, to assign over 400 police to keep order.

Within three years after the beginning of the campaign, the production of vodka, other liquors, and homebrew began to climb back up to pre-1985 levels. The campaign ended, for all intents and purposes, by 1988, because its supporters in the upper echelons of the party had been replaced, because people turned to dangerous alternatives, and because the decrease in alcohol taxes seriously depleted the treasury. Consumption of state-produced alcohol had temporarily dropped by an astounding 60 percent, but estimates that included the increase in the production of illegal homebrew showed a much smaller, yet still significant, overall decrease of 35 percent.

In the post-Soviet decades of the 1990s and 2000s, the government continued to wrestle with skyrocketing alcohol problems. Between 2009 and 2011, in an effort to curb drinking, the government raised the price of spirits by 10 percent, and the price of beer by over 300 percent. In 2010 the government prohibited the sale of alcohol in Moscow at night. Strict drinking and driving laws were put in place to stop alcohol-related accidents. Until 2011 the law maintained a zero tolerance policy regarding drinking and driving. In 2011 the government raised the legal blood–alcohol content slightly to 0.03 percent because people had complained that even those with hangovers who smelled of alcohol were being pulled over and arrested. Government vigilance did not fade, though, and in 2011 President Dmitry Medvedev signed a measure that would prohibit beer sales from kiosks by 2013, restrict alcohol advertising, and ban alcohol sales between 11 pm and 8 am. The state once again attempted to regulate the most popular commodity in Russia. Yet alcohol's centrality to Russian culture thwarted state efforts.

France

France was one of the wealthiest countries in the world in the early twenty-first-century, housing 39 of the global Fortune 500 companies. The global community, however, associated France with its signature product, wine. Multi-national wine corporations emerged in the 1980s to fill a worldwide demand, and by the turn of the twenty-first-century, the jump in demand by those in non-Western countries boosted wine sales even higher. In almost all societies drinking French wine bestowed prestige on those who purchased it. Within France wine punctuated the daily lives of the vast majority of the population. It structured meals, social events, and cultural rituals. Since wine permeated all segments of society, it was the consumption of other alcohol products, namely beer for the elite and cider for the working class, that signified class status. Moreover, the French identified drinking with masculinity, accepting higher rates of consumption by men as normal. Alcohol abuse by men did lead to higher rates of domestic violence in the late twentieth and early twenty-first-centuries, yet, while they did not condone it, the fact that society was not surprised by this correlation indicated an assumption about alcohol and masculinity.

Like many countries, France increased production of alcohol in the latter half of the twentieth-century. Following the Second World War the wine industry picked up after an earlier downturn. In the late twentieth-century global advertising contributed to its continued success. No longer was wine merely thought of as a part of daily sustenance in the families of the French, but in many areas of the world people thought of it as a status symbol. Consuming fine French wine became another way for the world's rich to demonstrate their cultural superiority.

By the 1980s deregulation in many countries led to another upturn in the global wine business. Global wine conglomerates emerged in the 1990s between French and Australian producers as well as between French and Californian producers. These conglomerates reflected the global nature of wine production at the end of the twentieth-century. Wine sales from France grew again in the first decade of the twenty-first-century because of increased demand from China and Russia for champagne and cognac. The United States, however, continued to lead the world in consumption of alcohol from France. The American market accounted for 22 percent of alcohol sales from France by 2006. France continued to expand its market share of global wine sales in the twenty-first-century. By 2010, for example, France was producing over 23 percent of the world's wine. International wine sales, then, exhibited the very characteristics of globalization that were so prevalent in other industries: deregulation, multi-national corporations, and production for a global market. In many ways the French wine business became an example for the internationalization of other industries. In France, as in other areas of the world, alcohol sales furthered the world trend of globalization.

Within France consumption of wine remained central to the lives of the people. In a survey taken in the mid-twentieth-century, almost 25 percent of the French had drunk some form of alcohol by the age of six, 41 percent by the age of nine, and 61 percent by the age of 12. Most people's early experiences likely entailed wine diluted by water and drunk with meals. By the time they were 18, almost 25 percent of the population had drunk to excess on at least one occasion. There were differences by gender, however. Females drank less than males, and more females abstained completely. Wine consumption in France did decline in the early twenty-first-century, however. For example, between 2001 and 2005 wine consumption in France dropped by 11 percent. Sidewalk cafés that served wine also declined in number as many people drank bottled water or liqueurs and spirits. Nevertheless, by 2007 the French still drank 64 liters a year of wine, much more than other countries.

Wine still remained France's most common drink; 90 percent of men and 56 percent of women drank wine daily by the end of the twentieth-century. Beer, cider, and spirits were consumed, but to a much lesser degree than wine. Yet beer and cider appeared to be class specific. The majority of the beer drinkers in France came from the upper-class, while those who drank cider came from the lower-class. Finally, far fewer people drank distilled spirits, and those spirits usually consisted of some form of brandy as an aperitif.

Many studies showed that abuse of alcohol remained relatively low for most of the twentieth-century in France. For example, in mid century 96 percent of women drank less than 16 ounces a day, while only 40 percent of men drank more than 16 ounces a day; 30 percent of the population did not drink daily. There were differences among classes, too. Agricultural laborers drank much more than other occupations, roughly one and a half times as much as business people. Moreover, as the educational scale lowered, the amount of alcohol increased. At mid century French society was very accepting of drinking, however. Certain specific beliefs contributed to this opinion. For example, people believed that drinking wine was good for those in heavy labor jobs because it was nourishing. They also believed that aperitifs aided digestion, warmed the body, and nicely complimented a meal. Society believed, however, that women should drink less than men. Overall, there was not much evidence that people believed one should not drink.

By the beginning of the twenty-first-century, however, some people argued that problem drinking was becoming a crisis in France. For example, a report written in 2005 by Hervé Chabalier, a prominent French journalist, claimed that France suffered from some serious problems with alcohol, even though society failed to acknowledge it ("'Alcoholism – The Simple Truth' – France." http://www.news-medical.net/news/2005/11/28/14713.aspx, accessed December 19, 2011). He reported that half of all domestic violence cases were associated with alcohol and a significant percentage of traffic accidents were alcohol related. Moreover, he asserted that 10 percent of the population suffered from an alcohol-related disease in the early twenty-first-century, and alcohol caused at least 23,000 deaths per year. He went on to say that the French also suffered from high levels of cirrhosis of the liver, and that France had two million alcoholics.

The French recognized problem drinkers as those who had a strong desire to drink, who had a hard time stopping, and whose drinking caused social or personal problems. Most heavy drinkers drank to excess between meals in cafés. Not all alcohol seemed to lead to problems, however. Many physicians in France did not believe that wine was problematic. For example, the two regions with the highest alcohol-related mortality rates, Normandy and Brittany, also had the lowest percentage of people who drank wine, the highest who drank cider, and the highest who drank distilled spirits. The regions with the highest rates of wine drinkers also had the lowest percentage of problem drinkers. Nevertheless, abuse and its incumbent problems did exist in France, which mirrored many other societies that also had cultures of abuse. Wine remained, however, central to France's cultural identity.

United States

Alcohol consumption in the United States rose throughout the twentieth- and early twenty-first-centuries, contributing to the role of the United States as the quintessential modern consumer society. Beer consumption increased with the introduction of beer cans and bottles in grocery stores, allowing people to drink privately without the social rituals associated with public alcohol venues, thus fostering the individualistic culture of the United States. In the globalized economy after the turn of the twenty-first-century, though, spirits consumption began to rise as global marketing of glamorous foreign liquors cultivated a high-end demand. Exotic spirits bestowed an elitist prestige on those with access to them, and brought especially non-Western cultures to the United States, exoticizing those cultures in the eyes of Americans.

Wine also grew as a status symbol in late twentieth-century America, deriving its demand from predominantly urban areas where people strove to be chic and urbane. Moreover, international marketing of American whiskey to developing countries successfully Westernized the tastes of consumers, providing them with an observable and relatively accessible way to welcome Western culture.

Within the United States alcohol consumption acted as a defining characteristic of identity. More men than women drank, and society defined prevalent alcohol consumption as an acceptable and widespread demonstration of masculinity. High levels of consumption by women, however, did not enhance, and in fact detracted from one's femininity. Moreover, the perceived alcohol habits of American ethnic groups led society to stereotype them, believing that alcohol overuse proved degeneracy, while moderation proved respectability. Abuse in the form of binge drinking by college-aged drinkers, however, somehow became socially acceptable as a normal right of passage.

American society was concerned with abuse, and gave birth to Alcoholics Anonymous in 1935. Alcoholics Anonymous helped popularize the disease concept of prolonged alcohol abuse, influencing the American Medical Association to add alcoholism to its lexicon of officially valid diseases, and indeed broadening the definition of disease itself. By the early twenty-first-century Alcoholics Anonymous had formed groups in the vast majority of countries, creating a worldwide ethos surrounding alcohol.

After the Volstead Act was repealed in 1933 alcohol production began to rise rapidly in the United States. By 1940 the level of beer production, for example, was back to the levels of the 1920s, although it was concentrated in the hands of fewer brewers. The sale of beer continued to increase throughout the war period of the early 1940s even though tin and malt needed for the war effort were scarce. Alcohol sales continued to climb throughout the rest of the twentieth-century and into the twenty-first-century.

Beer, spirits, and wine split the consumer alcohol market. Beer was the highest consumed alcohol at 53 percent, followed by spirits at 31 percent, and finally wine at 16 percent. Beer continued to be the most popular alcohol in the United States throughout the twentieth- and twenty-first-centuries. One reason could be that the price of beer as a percentage of income did not rise between the Second World War and the first decade of the twenty-first-century. Moreover, beer cans were introduced in the 1930s and beer bottles were introduced in the 1950s, so that it became much easier to purchase beer and drink it at home rather than having to go to a tavern to do so. Selling beer in six packs also made it easier to purchase beer for home use. Furthermore, the fact that it was sold in grocery and convenience stores made it easier to purchase and thus even more popular. By the early twenty-first-century 66 percent of all beer was purchased in six packs, whereas in the 1930s, for example, virtually all beer was drunk in taverns.

Spirits remained second to beer in their popularity, even though spirits consumption rose after 2000. For example, per capita consumption of spirits rose 9 percent between 2001 and 2005. And in 2005 alone sales of spirits increased 60 percent. Premium alcohol sales drove these changes. For example, several premium brands took over the top spots from less expensive brands during these years. Spirits companies also used exotic drinks to bring in the high-end alcohol market to the United States and abroad. Various kinds of cocktails such as the cosmo, sour apple martini, and mojito made their associated liquors popular. Other marketing tools such as specific shapes and colors of liquor bottles led consumers to buy more expensive spirits. The spirit that characterized the United States, however, was whiskey. In 2005, for example, whiskey sales rose by 24 percent in Asia, 19 percent in South America, and 89 percent in India, following a worldwide demand for American culture. In the early twenty-first-century these were new developing markets for worldwide advertising. Some researchers argue that part of the reason for the increase in sales both in the United States and abroad was television advertising. Trends in the international sale of spirits from the United States became emblematic of economic globalization in the early twenty-first-century.

Even though wine remained the third most popular drink in the United States, its consumption rose continuously between the Second World War and 2010. Wine became easily purchased by the bottle in many retail venues, which led to increased home consumption. Moreover, in 1991 when US news agencies reported that drinking wine, particularly red wine, could help stave off heart disease, the sale of wine increased 400 percent. It did decrease again after a few years, though. Unlike beer or spirits, drinking patterns for wine differed based on urbanization. By the early twenty-first-century 65 percent of wine was drunk in the largest 50 urban areas. In 2005, however, the Supreme Court ruled that wineries could ship their wine directly to consumers. This ruling began to change the demographics of wine consumption across the country, making boutique wine more accessible to a larger portion of the population. Even with this change, wine remained a status symbol with a largely urban customer base.

While the popularity of beer, spirits, and wine differed, differences also lay in general consumption patterns among people. In the early twenty-first-century in the United States consumption patterns ranged widely based on gender, venue, education, ethnicity, and age. For example, 71 percent of men in the United States drank, while 59 percent of women did. In addition, 75 percent of those with a college education drank while 50 percent of those with less than a high school education drank. Moreover, specific drinking patterns were used by groups to differentiate themselves from other social groups. Kinds of drinking establishments supported these differences. For example, drinking venues catered to specific clientele. Comedy clubs, dance clubs, breweries, martini bars, piano bars, rock music bars, gay/lesbian bars, neighborhood bars, and college bars all catered to specific groups of people.

Perhaps the most significant differences in drinking patterns existed among diverse ethnicities. More importantly, stereotypes regarding the drinking habits of certain ethnic groups served to further prejudice against those groups. Research, too, sometimes perpetuated racial stereotypes against ethnic minorities, especially African Americans, Asian Americans, and Hispanic Americans. By the early twenty-first-century, however, newer research showed that it was difficult to make generalizations about ethnic drinking patterns because tremendous variations existed among subgroups within ethnicities. For example, Mexican-American men had higher rates of heavy drinking as well as problems surrounding alcohol than did Puerto Rican-American men or Cuban-American men. In addition, Mexican-American women had both a higher rate of abstinence and a higher rate of heavy drinking than did Puerto Rican-American women or Cuban-American women.

Within white America many studies in the twentieth-century showed differences among sub-groups. Jewish Americans, for example, had fewer problems with drinking, even though they drank alcohol on social occasions as well as many religious occasions such as Rosh Hashanah, Passover, Hanukkah, Purim, and Yom Kippur. By the end of the twentieth-century, however, there was an increasing problem with excessive drinking among Jewish Americans, although they were still held up as examples of moderation. Other white ethnic groups were stereotyped as having more problems with excessive drinking. According to studies in the first half of the twentieth-century the white ethnic group with the highest percentage of problem drinking was Irish Americans. This research, however, became suspect in the later twentieth-century as prejudice against Irish Americans waned.

In the twentieth-century African Americans were also stereotyped as heavy drinkers. However, research that compared black males to white males showed this stereotype to be false. More black men abstained from alcohol than did white men; 36 percent compared to 26 percent respectively. Black men did drink more heavily in their forties and fifties while white men drank more in their twenties. Still, however, white males in their fifties drank more than black males in their fifties.

Asian Americans were typically stereotyped as low consumers of alcohol in the twentieth-century. As a whole they had lower consumption rates than the national average, but substantial differences arose within the group. Vietnamese Americans, and Chinese-Vietnamese Americans, had the highest levels of drinking, while Chinese Americans had the lowest. Japanese Americans, Filipino Americans, and Korean Americans were in the middle of the range. Japanese-American women had the highest rates of consumption, at 67 percent, while Korean-American women had the lowest, at 18 percent.

Researchers argue that the lower consumption rates of Asian Americans came from the flushing response, which was explained earlier in the discussion of China. Not all researchers, however, agreed with this explanation. Some argued that cultural rather than physiological reasons existed for lower drinking habits. These researchers asserted that Confucian and Taoist traditions that stressed harmony, conformity, and responsibility toward others caused lower consumption rates in first-generation Asian Americans. They went on to show that second- and third-generation Asian immigrants to the United States drank more than their first-generation parents or grandparents. Therefore, they reasoned that sociological rather than physiological differences better explained drinking habits.

One of the most widespread myths regarding alcohol consumption in the United States in the twentieth- and early twenty-first-centuries surrounded Native Americans' drinking habits. Native Americans were stereotyped as binge drinkers because of a supposed predisposition to abuse alcohol. Research, however, showed that the stereotype that Native Americans were physiologically and psychologically more apt to drink was false because so many differences in consumption patterns existed among the over five hundred tribes in the United States. Drinking stereotypes in the United States were a powerful tool used to further ethnic stereotypes in the twentieth and twenty-first-centuries.

While not an ethnic group, an important drinking subculture within the United States included youth up to age 25. Young people had specific problems with alcohol. Several research studies in the late twentieth- and early twenty-first centuries focused on underage as well as college-age binge drinking as a problem that needed a solution. Binge drinking could cause great harm and even death to those who participated in it. Some argued that binge drinking among youth was inevitable and therefore a policy of trying to curb the problem rather than a policy of trying to eliminate it would be more useful. Overall, drinking among youth decreased in the late twentieth and early twenty-first-centuries, yet binge drinking by those who did drink continued to cause a dangerous problem.

Binge drinking by young adults was only one of the forms of alcohol abuse that occurred in the United States. Alcoholism posed problems both in the twentieth- and early twenty-first-centuries. It afflicted those from dysfunctional as well as those from highly functional backgrounds. A study in the mid-twentieth century concluded that 18 percent of those from dysfunctional backgrounds were alcoholics, while 17 percent of those from functional backgrounds ended up as alcoholics. Alcoholics suffered from many health problems. Researchers knew that excessive use of ethanol, especially in the form of spirits, could cause malnutrition through the maldigestion and malabsorption of nutrients. In a heavy drinker alcohol might be the major form of caloric intake and therefore the drinker might not eat essential foods in his or her diet. Several diseases were associated with excessive alcohol consumption such as encephalopathies, liver problems, heart diseases, and nervous disorders. Deficiencies in vitamin B1 and vitamin B complex, which cause pellagra, dermatosis, digestive disorder, and mental dysfunction were found in heavy drinkers.

During the 1940s in the United States the belief in the disease concept of alcoholism became more widespread. By the first decade of the twenty-first-century the widely accepted viewpoint was that alcoholism was a disease, even though there were still those who believed it to be a personal failing. Within the disease school of alcoholism a question still existed in the early twenty-first-century of whether alcoholism was a mental or physical problem. Some argued that the disease concept was harmful because it implied that a medical "cure" could be found and therefore the psychological aspects were ignored. Others argued that alcoholism was both a physical and psychological disease and therefore required treatment from both fields of healthcare. When alcoholism became accepted as a health problem, or disease, people began to obtain health care coverage for treatment.

By the early twenty-first-century Alcoholics Anonymous was the most widespread organization helping alcoholics. Because there still existed extreme prejudice against alcoholics, the organization focused on anonymity. The AA program was based on a 12-step plan, which included things like admitting lack of control over addiction and making amends for mistakes made while still drinking. Some researchers in the early twenty-first-century, however, argued that AA worked no better than no treatment at all. Moreover, other groups argued that the idea of alcoholism was culturally constructed phenomenon rather than a specific disease. Therefore, because of differing cultural norms surrounding acceptable levels of drinking in the United States, it was ethnocentric to define any certain pattern of drinking as problem drinking. As a result, it became even more complicated to define alcohol issues, making treatment very difficult across ethnicities within the United States. Nonetheless, the Federal Government began to mandate both the availability of treatment programs for alcoholics, as well as their equal treatment under the law. In 1963 and then again in 1968, Congress specifically provided federal support to establish facilities for the treatment and rehabilitation of alcoholics. By 1973, alcoholism was defined as a disability, and alcoholics legally received "reasonable accommodation" at work and in many public places. Finally, in 1990 Congress passed the Americans

With Disabilities Act (ADA), which provided even broader protections for alcoholics who had gone through, or were participating in, alcohol rehabilitation.

Also, for the sake of public safety, the US sought to regulate the sale and use of alcohol after the end of Prohibition. The government limited sales through "blue laws", which restricted the days and times that alcohol could be sold. Moreover, several states passed laws setting the legal drinking age at 21. By 1984 the Federal Government enacted a "national minimum drinking age act," also setting the age at 21 and tying federal highway funds to compliance. By 1988 all states had passed the law. States also concentrated their efforts on drunk driving laws. Indiana passed the first drunk driving law in 1939, setting the blood–alcohol limit at .15. Subsequently, all states enacted drunk driving laws, and by 2004 all states had set .08 as the limit.

While regulation continued to concern the US it also realized the importance of alcohol taxes to the federal budget. One of the reasons the federal government repealed the Volstead Act, in fact, was the promise of alcohol taxes needed to help lift the country out of the depression. Since then the Federal as well as state and local governments have relied on excise taxes. Furthermore, by the end of 2011, after the US suffered a severe recession, several states increased alcohol taxes to make up deficits in their state budgets. Like many countries in the twentieth- and twenty-first-centuries, the US implicitly sought high alcohol sales – thus more tax revenues – far the sake of governmental budgets, blatantly contradicting its support of alcohol regulations for the sake of public safety. These political contradictions merely added to the already complex role of alcohol in economics, culture, and society in the twentieth- and twenty-first-century United States.

Conclusion

In the late twentieth- and early twenty-first-centuries, alcohol fed economic and cultural globalization. First, the international marketing of alcohol from all over the world promoted economic globalization. The rising demand for Latin American cachaça and tequila, Russian vodka and samogon, French wine, and US whiskey opened significant avenues of trade for those countries. Second, the alcohol trade facilitated the movement of Western and non-Western cultures globally. Western culture spread to non-Western areas such as Saudi Arabia, India, China, and Japan through the trade in Western alcohol. Western alcohol smuggled into Saudi Arabia met the increasing demand of elites, especially, to socialize over alcohol, bringing an aspect of Western culture to that country. In India the trade in "Indian-made foreign liquor" such as beer and spirits, and in China a jump in the sales of Western alcohol, provided a means with which to mimic Western culture to the growing number of people who wished to do so. In Japan the introduction of liquor in individually sized containers allowed drinkers to order separately rather than as a group, encouraging a Western sense of individualism. Alcohol production and trade also popularized non-Western culture, as Latin American cachaça and tequila, and Russian samogon spread in the West.

Alcohol consumption patterns helped culturally construct class, gender, and Western and non-Western identities globally. First, drinking patterns defined class identity in such diverse cultures as those found in Africa, Saudi Arabia, India, China, France, and the United States. In several African countries drinking bottled beer instead of indigenous beer signified upper- or middle-class status. In Saudi Arabia the clandestine use of Western liquor bespoke of elite privilege. Moreover, in India consumption of foreign liquors by elites furthered the cultural separation between the upper- and lower-classes, just as in China where drinking foreign alcohol as well as public displays of drunkenness indicated one's higher status within society. In France the upper class and the lower-class both had their signature drinks apart from wine that made up part of their identity; beer for the elites and cider for the lower-class. Finally, in the United States drinking wine became a status symbol, separating those who aspired to be elite from those in the lower-classes.

Third, drinking patterns further defined gender roles in many cultures. For example, men drank more alcohol in virtually every society, including those in Latin America, Africa, Saudi Arabia, China, Japan, Russia, France, and the United States. It became a well-known behavior associated with masculinity. In addition, statistics on Latin America, Russia, France, and the United States all revealed that drinking led to increased male violence, particularly in the home, reflecting society's expectations surrounding men, alcohol, and violence.

Fourth, the consumption of specific liquors bestowed a Western identity upon the consumer. Drinking bottled beer in Africa, Western spirits in India, and beer, whiskey, and wine in Japan overtly signified one's Westernness.

Fifth, the non-Western and rapidly developing societies of Latin America, Africa, India, China, and Japan (although Japan was relatively more developed), all confronted encroachment by an all-pervasive Western culture as they moved into the global economy. In response, many people in those countries maintained time-honored alcohol customs, displaying a visible and symbolic allegiance to traditional values and at least a partial rejection of Westernization.

Addressing the by-products of alcohol abuse in the later twentieth- and early twenty-first-centuries remained a goal of governments as well as civic societies around the world. First, the increase in drinking in the latter half of the twentieth-century resulted in increased alcohol abuse in many societies including Latin America, Saudi Arabia, India, Japan, Russia, France, and the United States. Rising levels of alcohol abuse caused major risks to public health and safety in the twentieth- and twenty-first-centuries. Violence in Latin America, Saudi Arabia, China, France, and the United States; a significant percentage of auto accidents in India, China, Russia, and the United States; skyrocketing mortality rates in Africa and Russia; and increases in mental as well as other chronic diseases in Saudi Arabia, India, France, and the United

States all resulted from alcohol abuse. Yet governments struggled to regulate alcohol. Regulations included such things as mandated legal drinking ages in Mexico, Japan, and the United States. The twentieth-century bore out the fact that prohibition, while perhaps temporarily decreasing consumption, did not eliminate it and instead led to the use of more dangerous forms of alcohol. The almost unanimous inability on the part of governments to have as much control over alcohol as they wanted, demonstrated the continued centrality of alcohol in people's lives. Alcohol's importance was also apparent in governments, as many countries, such as India, China, Japan, Russia, and the US, relied on alcohol taxes to help sustain their budgets. Second, outside of government, Alcoholics Anonymous groups spread out from the United States to virtually every corner of the globe, including Latin America, Africa, Saudi Arabia, India, and China. AA disseminated the Western ideology that alcoholism was a disease and then offered a 12-step plan to recovery. While it adapted to other cultures, AA still brought with it Western beliefs that permeated non-Western societies.

The trade, use, abuse, and regulation of alcohol in the twentieth- and twenty-first-centuries defined people's lives in many ways. Its high demand worldwide opened markets for several countries, earning them both profits from the trade as well as national identities associated with their signature alcohol. Alcohol helped spread Western and non-Western cultures to many parts of the world, while it signified class and social status as well as ethnic and gender identities within societies. Its ubiquitous nature ensured its continued importance into the twenty-first-century.

Further reading

AbuMadini, M. S., Sheikh I. A. Rahim, M. A. Al-Zahrani, and A. O. Al-Johi. 2008. "Two decades of Treatment Seeking for Substance Use Disorders in Saudi Arabia: Trends and Patterns in a Rehabilitation Facility in Dammam." *Drug and Alcohol Dependence.* (97): 231–36.

Albrithen, A. A. 2006 "Alcoholism and Domestic Violence in Saudi Society." PhD Dissertation University of Liverpool.

AlMarri, T. 2009. "Alcohol and Substance Use in the Arabian Gulf Region: A Review." *International Journal of Psychology.* 44 (3): 222–33.

Anderson, K. 1995. *Young People and Alcohol, Drugs and Tobacco.* Finland: World Health Organization.

Anderson, K. (ed.) 2004. *The World's Wine Markets: Globalization at Work.* Cheltenham: Edward Elgar.

Babor, T. F. 1986. *Alcohol and Culture: Comparative Perspectives from Europe and America.* New York: New York Academy of Sciences.

Barr, A. 1999. *Drink: A Social History of America.* New York: Carroll & Graf Publishers.

Blaine, A. (ed.) 1980. *Alcoholism and the Jewish Community.* New York: Commission on Synagogue Relations, Federation of Jewish Philanthropies of New York.

Caetano, R., C. L. Clark, and T. Tam. 1998. "Alcohol Consumption Among Ethnic Minorities, Theory and Research." *Alcohol Health & Research World.* 22 (4): 233–41.

Chaudron, C. D. and D. A. Wilkinson (eds.) 1988. *Theories on Alcoholism.* Toronto: Addiction Research Foundation.

Dorschner, J. P. 1981. *Alcohol Consumption in a Village in North India.* Studies in Cultural Anthropology, NO. 1. Ann Arbor, MI: UMI Research Press.

Eber, C. 1995. *Women & Alcohol in a Highland Maya Town: Water of Hope, Water of Sorrow.* Austin: University of Texas Press.

Ewing, J. A. and B. A. Rouse. 1978. *Drinking: Alcohol in American Society – Issues and Current Research.* Chicago: Nelson-Hall.

Gastineau, C., W. J. Darby, and T. B. Turner (eds.) 1979. *Fermented Food Beverages in Nutrition.* New York: Academic Press.

Gefou-Madianou, D. (ed.) 1992. *Alcohol, Gender and Culture.* New York: Routledge.

Giesbrecht, N., R. Room, E. Oesterberg, J. Moskalewicz, and M. Cahannes (eds.) 1983. "Consequences of Drinking, Trends in Alcohol Problem Statistics in Seven Countries." Papers associated with Alcohol, Society, and the State – a report of the International Study of Alcohol Control Experiences, in collaboration with the World Health Organization Regional Office for Europe. Toronto: Addiction Research Foundation.

Graham, K. and R. Homel. 2008. *Raising the Bar: Preventing Aggression in and Around Bars, Pubs, and Clubs.* Portland, OR: Willan Publishing.

Grant, M. 1998. *Alcohol and Emerging Markets: Patterns, Problems, and Responses.* Philadelphia: Brunner/Mazel.

Grant, M. and J. Litvak. 1998. *Drinking Patterns and Their Consequences.* Washington, DC: Taylor & Francis.

Hao W., J. Derson, S. Xiao, L. Li, and L. Zhang 1999. "Alcohol Consumption and Alcohol-Related Problems: Chinese experience from Six Area Samples, 1994." *Addiction.* 94 (10): 1467–76.

Hauge, R. 1984. *Alcohol and Crime.* Strasbourg: Council of Europe.

Heath, D. B. 1987. "Anthropology and Alcohol Studies: Current Issues." *Annual Review of Anthropology.* (16): 99–142.

——2000. *Drinking Occasions, Comparative Perspectives on Alcohol and Culture.* Series on Alcohol in Society. International Center for Alcohol Policies. Ann Arbor, MI: Sheridan Books.

Helzer, J. E. and G. J. Canino. (eds.) 1992. *Alcoholism in North America, Europe, and Asia.* New York: Oxford University Press.

Hiramani, A. B. and N. Sharma. 1988. *Health and Youth in India.* Delhi: Agam Prakashan.

Jones, A., W. D. Connor, and D. E. Powell (eds.) 1991. *Soviet Social Problems.* Boulder, CO: Westview Press.

Kirkby, D. 1998. *Barmaids: A History of Women's Work in Pubs.* New York: Cambridge University Press.

Kueny, K. 2001. *The Rhetoric of Sobriety: Wine in Early Islam.* Albany: State University of New York Press.

Lehto, J. 1995. *Approaches to Alcohol Control Policy.* Copenhagen: World Health Organization.

Leon, D. A., V. M. Shkolnikow, and M. Mckee. 2009. "Alcohol and Russian Mortality: A Continuing Crisis." *Addiction.* 104 (10) (October): 1630–36.

Lin, T. and D. T. Lin. 1982. "Alcoholism among the Chinese: Further observations of a low-risk population." *Culture, Medicine and Psychiatry.* 6 (2): 109–16.

Manheimer, A. (ed.) 2007. *Alcohol.* New York: Thomson Gale.

Maternovsky, D. and M. Sysoyeva. 2011. "Medvedev Signs Law Restricting Russian Beer, Alcohol Sales." *Bloomberg News.* http://www.bloomberg.com/news/2011-7-20/medvedev-signs-law-restricting-russian-beer-alcohol-sales-1-.html (accessed September 2, 2011).

McDonald, M. (ed.) 1994. *Gender, Drink and Drugs.* New York: Berg.

McGovern, P. E. 2009. *Uncorking the Past: The Quest for Wine, Beer and Other Alcoholic Beverages.* Berkeley: University of California Press.

Michalak, L. and K. Trocki. 2006. "Alcohol and Islam: An Overview." *Contemporary Drug Problems.* 33 (4) (Winter): 523–62.

Minai, K. 1986. *Trends in Alcoholic Beverage Consumption in Postwar Japan: An Analysis and Interpretation of Aggregate Data.* Singapore: Department of Japanese Studies National University of Singapore.

Peele, S. and M. Grant. 1999. *Alcohol and Pleasure: A Health Perspective.* Philadelphia: Brunner/Mazel.

Pernanen, K. 1991. *Alcohol in Human Violence.* New York: The Guilford Press.

Phillips, R. 2000. *A Short History of Wine.* New York: Harper Collins.

Roberts, B. D. 2000. "Always Cheaply Pleasant: Beer as Commodity in a Rural Kenyan Society." In *Commodities and Globalization, Anthropological Perspectives.* A. Haugerud, M. P. Stone, and P. D. Little (eds.) New York: Rowman & Littlefield.

Room, R. 1984. "Alcohol and Ethnography: A Case of Problem Deflation?" *Current Anthropology.* 25 (2): 169–91.

Rothbaum, N. 2007. *The Business of Spirits: How Savvy Marketers, Innovative Distillers, and Entrepreneurs Changed How We Drink.* New York: Kaplan.

Saul, M. 1981. "Beer, Sorghum and Women: Production for the Market in Rural Upper Volta." *Africa.* 51 (3): 746–64.

Single, E., P. Morgan, and J. de Lint (eds.) 1981. *Alcohol, Society, and the State: The Social History of Control Policy in Seven Countries.* Toronto: Addition Research Foundation and World Health Organization.

Smith, S. R. 1992. "Drinking Etiquette in a Changing Beverage Market." In *Re-Made in Japan.* J. J. Tobin (ed.) New Haven, CT: Yale University Press.

Snyder, C. R. 1958. *Alcohol and the Jews: A Cultural Study of Drinking and Sobriety.* New Haven, CT: Yale Center of Alcohol Studies.

White, S. 1996. *Russia Goes Dry: Alcohol, State and Society.* Cambridge: Cambridge University Press.

Wong, G. 2009. "Russia's Bleak Picture of Health." CNN.com/health. May 19. http://edition.cnn.com/2009/HEALTH/05/19/russia.health/index.html (accessed September 2, 2011).

Zhang, F.-P. 1982. "Drinking in China." *The Drinking and Drug Practices Surveyor.* 18: 12–15.

8 Conclusion

Continuity rather than change characterizes the story of alcohol over time and across civilizations. From even earlier than the beginnings of agriculture to the twenty-first-century alcohol shaped the cultural, social, political, and economic spheres of societies. It structured rituals and celebrations. It spread culture, and it also preserved culture in the face of social and political change. Alcohol furthered social differences such as class, ethnicity, and gender, and it prompted one of the most important social movements of the nineteenth-century in many Western countries, temperance. Alcohol regulation effectively controlled segments of society, and its taxes bolstered governments by bringing in significant revenues. Colonial governments used alcohol as a tool to further oppress the colonized, and the colonized used alcohol to resist oppressive governments. Finally, through trade, especially international trade, alcohol helped economies flourish. In essence, alcohol defined cultures, signified social differentiation, funded political structures, and stimulated economic development.

Alcohol possessed symbolic meanings from the time of the ancient civilizations into the twenty-first-century. In virtually every society it was central to rights of passage and it shaped important rituals. It symbolized the hospitality of hosts, the coming together of families in marriage, and the passing of life into death. Moreover, alcohol held symbolic meanings in the world's organized religions. Its use shaped the way religious ceremonies took place in Judaism and Christianity, and its regulation defined the fundamental principles of Islam and Buddhism.

Alcohol was a medium through which culture spread, or conversely, a medium to maintain traditions in the face of cultural infiltration. The expansion of alcohol into new areas changed social interactions and rituals. For example, the classical Greeks extended their culture to the colonies in Italy through viticulture and viniculture. In the late Classical and Post-Classical periods organized religions across the globe used alcohol to solidify their cultural impact by either introducing new alcohol rituals or by banning alcohol outrightly. In pre-colonial Latin America the Incas successfully co-opted conquered groups by establishing their own corn beer, or chicha, rituals in the newly conquered areas.

In modern world history Western culture permeated non-Western cultures through alcohol. For example, in the sixteenth-century Spanish drinking habits migrated to Latin America with colonization, not only changing indigenous cultures but also causing social unrest. In the nineteenth-century Western alcohol customs infiltrated Africa through colonization, transforming indigenous life and in some cases causing social breakdown. In both cases, however, indigenous groups did not completely succumb, rather they continued to practice alcohol traditions as a way to stave off Western cultural influences. In the twentieth-century, US culture permeated Japan through new drinking practices, while at the same time the Japanese used Western alcohol to continue established cultural traditions. Finally, in the late twentieth-century the culture of alcoholism as a disease spread from Western to non-Western societies such as China and India, augmenting their definitions of disease.

Alcohol helped shape societies. It was a vital nutritional ingredient in the daily lives of most agriculturally based groups, and it helped define medicine in many societies from the Pre-Classical period up through the twenty-first-century. One of the most important social roles that alcohol played, however, was to signify or sometimes even grant status within societies. In ancient and Classical civilizations people gained status through providing alcohol for feasts, which gave them tremendous social capital. In Classical Greek society elites especially labeled people based on the type of alcohol they drank. Drinking diluted wine, according to elites, distinguished them from others, while drinking beer and undiluted wine demonstrated one's lower class status. Alcohol consumption patterns continued to denote class in modern history. Wine, for example, was a status symbol in many societies. In colonial Latin America elite Spaniards flaunted their status by drinking wine, while the indigenous lower classes drank pulque. In early-modern Britain elites drank wine and the lower classes drank ale, and in nineteenth-century Ireland the gentry drank wine, while the lower-classes drank whiskey and beer. In the twentieth and early twenty-first-century West, wine remained a status symbol. Other alcohols, too, were used to display status in the twentieth- and early twenty-first-centuries. In modern India, Western whiskey was a status symbol, and in modern Africa drinking bottled beer became a sign of middle-class status. In the twenty-first-century West, drinking exotic indigenous alcohols from non-Western countries conferred a status of exclusivity on the usually young, urban professionals who drank them.

Drinking privileges and venues also separated elites and commoners. For example, the ancient Egyptians and later the pre-colonial Aztecs both allowed elites the privilege of drinking to excess, while they punished commoners for such behavior. In the twenty-first-century the Chinese began to accept public drunkenness by elites even though such behavior violated social mores. Drinking venues in modern societies also furthered the differentiation among classes. This was especially true in the West. In nineteenth-century France cafés specialized in serving either the elite or the working-class, and in industrializing Britain private clubs served elites while many pubs catered only to the working-class. Separation of drinking venues by class continued into the twenty-first-century.

Other social differences were defined by alcohol consumption patterns as well. During the formation of Islam Muslims visibly set themselves apart from Christians by abstaining from alcohol. Christians, too, created new alcohol rituals to set themselves apart from pagans. People continued to use alcohol in modern history to prove social differentiation, and even to reinforce stereotypes. In the twentieth-century United States, for example, mainstream beliefs about ethnic drinking patterns fueled prejudice. Negative stereotypes of Irish Americans, African Americans, and Native Americans were justified by labeling them as alcohol abusers, while positive stereotypes of Asian Americans were furthered by the belief that they were prudent in their alcohol consumption habits. It was true that each ethnic group represented certain trends in alcohol consumption, yet within ethnic groups widely varying alcohol habits existed. Moreover, in the twentieth- and early twenty-first-century United States various subcultures used alcohol venues to affirm their shared identity. Gay and lesbian bars, college bars, country and western bars, and neighborhood bars all exemplified this pattern.

Alcohol reinforced and at times defined gender identity. Both alcohol production as well as consumption patterns helped to strengthen gender roles. In many agricultural societies women were responsible for producing alcohol. In pre-colonial Incan society, for example, only women made chicha. Since chicha was a sacred element, as well as central to daily nutrition, making it strengthened women's status in that society. Moreover, as civilizations developed into market societies and alcohol became a commodity, women kept their roles as alcohol producers and began selling it, gaining some economic independence as a result. For example, in medieval Britain many women made their livings by producing and selling alcohol. The same was true in Latin America and Africa. In many cases, however, with the onset of mass production, the alcohol trade moved away from cottage industry and became a big business. Men took over its production and sale, identifying the industry as masculine, and economically marginalizing many women as a result. This happened in early-modern Britain and later on in many parts of Africa. In parts of Latin America, however, chicha remained popular, and its production stayed predominantly in the hands of women in cottage industry, showing that in the areas where an indigenous alcohol culture remained, women continued to hold economically strong roles by selling alcohol.

Many cultures, however, severely limited women's access to alcohol. In Rome, for example, during the Greco-Roman period men were said to kiss their wives upon arrival for the sole purpose of detecting alcohol on their breath, and some women were even killed by their families for drinking alcohol. In Classical India the *Kama Sutra* forbade wives to drink alcohol, but allowed mistresses, whose sexual reputation was already tainted, to do so. Modern societies, even into the twentieth-century, virtually banned women from drinking in public venues. Those who did risked being labeled as prostitutes. Societies imbued alcohol with so much power to define women that association with it could ruin or even kill a woman.

Men's gender identity was defined by their relationship to alcohol as well. In Australia up until the late-twentieth-century, pubs were bastions of white male power as well as centers of political activity. Pubs epitomized masculinity, and acted as centers of political power in that country, effectively emasculating aboriginal men who were banned from them, and excluding aborigines as well as women from politics. In the late twentieth-century, however, it became legal for aborigines to drink in pubs and more acceptable for women to do so. Acquiring these rights was so momentous that women viewed their ability to finally enter pubs as even more important than their right to vote. Beliefs surrounding alcohol and gender began to shift toward the end of the twentieth-century, but older stereotypes likely still influenced male and female behavior. In the United States, for example, at the end of the twentieth century 71 percent of men drank while 59 percent of women did so.

Reinforcing and sometimes creating identity was not the only way alcohol influenced society. Alcohol prompted a powerful, international social movement in the nineteenth- and early-twentieth-centuries. Temperance arose largely in Western, Protestant countries ostensibly as a response to the upsurge in alcohol consumption brought on by the tremendous social changes accompanying industrialization. It became, however, an effective means for the powerful as well as the oppressed to further their social and political agendas. For example, in nineteenth-century Ireland the Protestant minority used temperance ideology to justify their political and social control over the marginalized Catholic majority, who they deemed irresponsible drunkards. In the United States widely held temperance beliefs gave the elite and the middle class a moral rationale for the poor conditions of both ethnic minorities and the urban working class. They labeled these marginalized groups as alcohol abusers, successfully deflecting the focus away from structural inequality. Marginalized groups also embraced temperance, however. Catholics in nineteenth-century Ireland and African Americans in the nineteenth-century United States both advocated for temperance within their own groups as a way to prove their high moral character, thus justifying their arguments for equality.

Governments, too, used alcohol to further their agendas. Virtually all governments regulated alcohol in some way. Alcohol regulation, however, became more than a means to protect public health and safety. It played three important roles in society. First, governments used liquor laws as a tool to reinforce the social hierarchy, directing most of the regulations at the lower classes and the socially marginalized. Liquor laws effectively controlled the behavior of these groups and reinforced their lack of power. For example, the Aztecs highly curtailed the consumption of alcohol by commoners and punished them severely if they did not comply. In colonial Latin America the Spanish government repeatedly passed laws to regulate indigenous drinking. The same was true in industrializing Britain where the government regulated gin consumption, a favorite of the working-class, and in nineteenth-century Ireland where the government regulated whiskey, also a drink of the lower class. Second, governments regulated alcohol venues as a way to maintain political control. Governments from Mesopotamia, to the colonial Americas, to nineteenth-century France all believed that drinking establishments were dangerous centers of political intrigue, fearing that political agitators gathered in these places to foment rebellion.

Third, even though governments regulated alcohol, they also took advantage of its popularity. Some of the same governments that attempted to limit the consumption of alcohol by the lower classes also used it as a way to induce that same segment of society to work for the benefit of the government. In sixteenth-century colonial Latin America and in nineteenth-century colonial Africa, for example, the governments paid indigenous workers in alcohol to work in the mines and to build large infrastructure projects. Moreover, many governments brought in significant tax revenues from the alcohol trade. These monies provided the means for the growth and maintenance of their political structures. For example, alcohol taxes played a large role in sustaining the governments of ancient Egypt, early-modern Britain, colonial Latin America, nineteenth-century Russia, and twentieth-century colonial Africa. By the nineteenth-century, Russian alcohol taxes accounted for 30 percent of their total tax revenues, and in twentieth-century colonial Nigeria alcohol taxes accounted for 75 percent of that government's revenue. These many regulations as well as taxes show that governments recognized the power of alcohol and its venues to destabilize as well as sustain political and social structures.

Indigenous groups struggling for political autonomy also understood the power of alcohol in politics. They believed that gaining control over alcohol use symbolized independence. This was the case in India in the nineteenth and early-twentieth-centuries where the independence movement pushed for prohibition, which was seen as a break away from the British colonial alcohol culture, and in South Africa later in the century where native Africans rioted to abolish the beerhall system, a hated symbol of apartheid.

In many societies alcohol played a role in their economic success. In these societies alcohol accounted for a sizable portion of trade, and sometimes even drove economic growth. In ancient Mesopotamia, for example, the wine trade was predominantly responsible for developing crucial trading networks. In Europe in the early-modern period wine accounted for 30 percent of all English imports and 25 percent of all imports to the Low Countries. Moreover, during the formation of the modern world system wine was a valuable commodity for the powerful Dutch traders, and its widespread demand allowed Portugal to expand its trading networks to many parts of the world. Furthermore, the African demand for alcohol during the Atlantic slave trade helped to make that system work. For example, it paid for 25 percent of all the slaves from Angola. Even after the end of the Atlantic slave trade Europe sold alcohol to Africa in exchange for raw materials crucial to European industry. In the late-twentieth- and early-twenty-first-centuries alcohol became important in international trade agreements. Mexico in one agreement and Brazil in another demanded sole ownership of the names of popular liquors that had originated in their countries. Their success set precedents for international laws regarding intellectual property rights. Finally, in the late-twentieth century the value of alcohol as a commodity could be seen in the significant advertising space it commanded. In China, for example, alcohol producers spent almost 20 percent of all their television advertising budgets on liquor ads.

Alcohol has had a presence in almost all civilizations. Its physiological properties as well as its symbolism have smoothed the path for human interactions in cultural, social, political, and economic settings. It has shaped cultures both where it has been used and where it has been banned. Control over its use has provided social as well as political power. And its economic value has made it an important commodity in the domestic as well as the international trade of many societies. Its meanings as well as its uses have been myriad, making its influence omnipresent in human history.

Bibliography

AbuMadini, M. S., Sheikh I. A. Rahim, M. A. Al-Zahrani, and A. O. Al-Johi. 2008. "Two Decades of Treatment Seeking for Substance Use Disorders in Saudi Arabia: Trends and Patterns in a Rehabilitation Facility in Dammam." *Drug and Alcohol Dependence* (97): 231–36.

AlMarri, T. 2009. "Alcohol and Substance Use in the Arabian Gulf Region: A Review." *International Journal of Psychology* 44 (3): 222–33.

Ambler, C. H. 1987. *Alcohol and Disorder in Pre-Colonial Africa.* Working Papers in African Studies No. 126. Boston: African Studies Center, Boston University.

Ancient Egyptian Medicine: The Papyrus Ebers. 1930. Trans. C. P. Bryan. Chicago: Ares Publishers.

Anderson, K. 1995. *Young People and Alcohol, Drugs and Tobacco.* Finland: World Health Organization.

Anderson, K. (ed.) 2004. *The World's Wine Markets: Globalization at Work.* Cheltenham: Edward Elgar.

Babor, T. F. 1986. *Alcohol and Culture: Comparative Perspectives from Europe and America.* New York: New York Academy of Sciences.

Barr, A. 1999. *Drink: A Social History of America.* New York: Carroll & Graf Publishers.

Barrows, S. and R. Room. (eds.) 1991. *Drinking Behavior and Belief in Modern History.* Berkeley: University of California Press.

Bennett, J. M. 1996. *Ale, Beer, and Brewsters in England: Women's Work in a Changing World, 1300–1600.* New York: Oxford University Press.

Bennett, L. A. 1984. "Ethnography, Alcohol, and South-Central European Societies." A dedicated issue of articles in the *East European Quarterly* 18, no. 4.

Bennett, L. A. and G. M. Ames. 1985. *The American Experience with Alcohol: Contrasting Cultural Perspectives.* New York: Plenum Press.

Berger, P. 1985. *The Art of Wine in East Asia.* San Francisco: Asian Art Museum of San Francisco.

Blaine, A. (ed.) 1980. *Alcoholism and the Jewish Community.* New York: Commission on Synagogue Relations, Federation of Jewish Philanthropies of New York.

Bledsoe, C. and G. Pison. (eds.) 1994. *Nuptiality in Sub-Saharan Africa: Contemporary Anthropological and Demographic Perspectives.* Oxford: Clarendon Press.

Bowen, H. V., M. Lincoln, and N. Rigby. 2002. *The Worlds of the East India Company.* Rochester, New York: The Boydell Press.

Bruman, H. J. 2000. *Alcohol in Ancient Mexico.* Salt Lake City: University of Utah Press.

Bryceson, D. F. (ed.) 2002. *Alcohol in Africa: Mixing Business, Pleasure, and Politics.* Portsmouth, NH: Heinemann.

Caetano, R., C. L. Clark, and T. Tam. 1998. "Alcohol Consumption Among Ethnic Minorities, Theory and Research." *Alcohol Health & Research World* 22 (4): 233–41.

Carlson, R. G. 1990. "Banana Beer, Reciprocity, and Ancestor Propitiation Among the Haya of Bukoba, Tanzania." *Ethnology* 29 (4): 297–311.

Chaudron, C. D. and D. A. Wilkinson. (eds.) 1988. *Theories on Alcoholism.* Toronto: Addiction Research Foundation.

Clark, P. 1983. *The English Alehouse: a social history, 1200–1830.* New York: Longman.

Colson, E. and T. Scudder. 1988. *For Prayer and Profit: The Ritual, Economic, and Social Importance of Beer in Gwembe District, Zambia, 1950–1982.* Standford, CA: Stanford University Press.

Crush, J. and C. Ambler (eds.) 1992. *Liquor and Labor in Southern Africa.* Athens: Ohio University Press.

Curto, J. 1996. *Alcohol and Slaves: The Luso-Brazilian Alcohol Commerce at Mpinda, Luanda, and Benguela during the Atlantice Slave trade c. 1480–1830 and its Impact on the Societies of West Central Africa.* PhD Dissertation University of California Los Angeles.

——2006. *Enslaving Spirits: The Portuguese-Brazilian Alcohol Trade at Luanda and its Hinterland, c. 1550–1830.* Boston, MA: Brill.

Darby, W. J. P. G. and L. Grivetti. 1976. *Food: The Gift of Osiris.* Vol. 2. London: Academic Press.

Davies, W. W. 1905. *The Codes of Hammurabi and Moses.* Cincinnati: Jennings and Graham.

Dayagi-Mendels, M. 1999. *Drink and Be Merry: Wine and Beer in Ancient Times.* Jerusalem: The Israel Museum.

Dietler, M. and B. Hayden. (eds.) 2001. *Feasts: Archaeological and Ethnographic Perspectives on Food, Politics, and Power.* Washington, DC: Smithsonian Institution Press.

Dorschner, J. P. 1981. *Alcohol Consumption in a Village in North India.* Studies in Cultural Anthropology, No. 1. Ann Arbor, MI: UMI Research Press.

Duis, P. R. 1983. *The Saloon: Public Drinking in Chicago and Boston 1880–1920.* Urbana: University of Illinois Press.

Eber, C. 1995. *Women & Alcohol in a Highland Maya Town: Water of Hope, Water of Sorrow.* Austin: University of Texas Press.

Ewing, J. A. and B. A. Rouse. 1978. *Drinking: Alcohol in American Society – Issues and Current Research.* Chicago: Nelson-Hall.

Forbes, R. J. 1948. *Short History of the Art of Distillation: from the Beginnings up to the Death of Cellier Blumenthal.* Leiden: E. J. Brill.

Gastineau, C., W. J. Darby, and T. B. Turner (eds.) 1979. *Fermented Food Beverages in Nutrition.* New York: Academic Press.

Gately, I. 2009. *Drink: A Cultural History of Alcohol.* New York: Gotham.

Gefou-Madianou, D. (ed.) 1992. *Alcohol, Gender and Culture.* New York: Routledge.

Geller, J. 1993. "Bread and Beer in Fourth-Millennium Egypt." *Food and Foodways* 5 (3): 255–67.

Giesbrecht, N., R. Room, E. Oesterberg, J. Moskalewicz, and M. Cahannes (eds.) 1983. *Consequences of Drinking, Trends in Alcohol Problem Statistics in Seven Countries. Papers associated with Alcohol, Society, and the State – a report of the International Study of Alcohol Control Experiences, in collaboration with the World*

Health Organization Regional Office for Europe. Toronto: Addiction Research Foundation.

Gordon, E. 1913. *The Anti-Alcohol Movement in Europe.* New York: Fleming H. Revell Company.

Graham, K. and R. Homel. 2008. *Raising the Bar: Preventing Aggression in and Around Bars, Pubs, and Clubs.* Portland, OR: Willan Publishing.

Grant, M. 1958. *Chinese Civilizaation.* Trans. K. E. Innes and M. R. Brailsford. New York: Meridian Books, Inc.

——1998. *Alcohol and Emerging Markets: Patterns, Problems, and Responses.* Philadelphia: Brunner/Mazel.

Grant, M. and J. Litvak. 1998. *Drinking Patterns and Their Consequences.* Washington, DC: Taylor & Francis.

Gutzke, D. W. 1996. *Alcohol in the British Isles from Roman Times to 1996: An Annotated Bibliography.* Westport, CT: Greenwood Press.

Hackwood, F. W. 1985. *Inns, Ales and Drinking Customs of Old England.* London: Bracken Books.

Haine, W. S. 1996. *The World of the Paris Café, Sociability Among the French Working Class, 1789–1914.* Baltimore, MD: Johns Hopkins University Press.

Hao Wei, Y. Derson, S. Xiao, L. Li, and Y. Zhang 1999. "Alcohol Consumption and Alcohol-Related Problems: Chinese experience from Six Area Samples, 1994." *Addiction* 94 (10): 1467–76.

Hartman, L. F. and A. L. Oppenheim. 1950. "On Beer and Brewing Techniques in Ancient Mesopotamia." *Journal of the American Oriental Society* 10: 1–55.

Hauge, R. 1984. *Alcohol and Crime.* Strasbourg: Council of Europe.

Haworth, A. 1995. "Zambia." In D. B. Heath (ed.) *International Handbook on Alcohol and Culture.* Westport, CT: Greenwood Press.

Heath, D. B. 1987. "Anthropology and Alcohol Studies: Current Issues." *Annual Review of Anthropology* 16: 99–142.

——2000. *Drinking Occasions, Comparative Perspectives on Alcohol and Culture.* Series on Alcohol in Society Published by the International Center for Alcohol Policies. Ann Arbor, MI: Sheridan Books.

——(ed.) 1995. *International Handbook on Alcohol and Culture.* Westport, CT: Greenwood Press.

Heath, D. B. and A. M. Cooper. 1981. *Alcohol Use and World Cultures: A Comprehensive Bibliography of Anthropological Sources.* Bibliographic Series No. 15. Toronto: Addiction Research Foundation.

Helzer, J. E. and G. J. Canino. (eds.) 1992. *Alcoholism in North America, Europe, and Asia.* New York: Oxford University Press.

Hewitt, T. F. 1980. *A Biblical Perspective on the Use and Abuse of Alcohol and Other Drugs.* Raleigh, NC: Pastoral Care Council on Alcohol and Drug Abuse.

Hiramani, A. B. and N. Sharma. 1988. *Health and Youth in India.* Delhi: Agam Prakashan.

Hyams, E. 1965. *Dionysus: A Social History of the Wine Vine.* New York: The Macmillian Company.

Jankowiak, W. and D. Bradburd. (eds.) 2003. *Drugs, Labor, and Colonial Expansion.* Tucson: University of Arizona Press.

Jennings, J. 2005. "La Chichera y El Patrón: Chicha and the Energetics of Feasting in the Prehistoric Andes." *Archaeological Papers of the American Anthropological Association* 14: 241–59.

Joffe, A. H. 1998. "Alcohol and Social Complexity in Ancient Western Asia." *Current Anthropology* 39 (3): 297–322.

Jones, A., W. D. Connor, and D. E. Powell. (eds.) 1991. *Soviet Social Problems.* Boulder, CO: Westview Press.

Kicza, J. E. 1980. "The Pulque Trade of Late Colonial Mexico City." *The Americas* 37 (2): 193–221.

Kirkby, D. 1997. *Barmaids: A History of Women's Work in Pubs.* Cambridge: Cambridge University Press.

Kueny, K. 2001. *The Rhetoric of Sobriety: Wine in Early Islam.* Albany: State University of New York Press.

Kunio, Y. 1957. *Japanese Manners and Customs in the Meiji Era.* Trans. C. S. Terry. Tokyo: Obunsha.

La Hausse, P. 1988. *Brewers, Beerhalls and Boycotts: A history of Liquor in South Africa.* History Workshop Booklet. Johannesburg: Ravan.

Lehto, J. 1995. *Approaches to Alcohol Control Policy.* Copenhagen: World Health Organization.

Lemu, B. A. 1992. *Islam and Alcohol.* Alexandria: Saadawi Publications.

Leon, D. A., V. M. Shkolnikow, and M. Mckee. 2009. "Alcohol and Russian Mortality: A Continuing Crisis." *Addiction* 104 (10) (October): 1630–36.

Lin, T. and D. T. Lin. 1982. "Alcoholism among the Chinese: Further observations of a low-risk population." *Culture, Medicine and Psychiatry* 6 (2):109–16.

Lucia, S. P., M.D. 1963. *A History of Wine As Therapy.* Philadelphia: J. B. Lippincott Company.

Lutz, H. F. 1922. *Viticulture and Brewing in The Ancient Orient.* New York: G. E. Stechert & Co.

MacAndrew, C. and B. R. Edgerton 1969. *Drunken Comportment: A Social Explanation.* Chicago: Aldine Publishing Company.

Malcolm, E. 1986. *"Ireland Sober, Ireland Free" Drink and Temperance in Nineteenth-Century Ireland.* Syracuse, NY: Syracuse University Press.

Manheimer, A. (ed.) 2007. *Alcohol.* New York: Thomson Gale.

Martin, A. L. 2001. *Alcohol, Sex, and Gender in Late Medieval and Early Modern Europe.* New York: Palgrave.

Maternovsky, D. and M. Sysoyeva. 2011. "Medvedev Signs Law Restricting Russian Beer, Alcohol Sales." *Bloomberg News.* http://www.bloomberg.com/news/2011-7-20/medvedev-signs-law-restricting-russian-beer-alcohol-sales-1-.html (accessed September 2, 2011).

McAllister, P. 2001. *Building the Homestead: Agriculture, Labour and Beer in South Africa's Transkei.* Leiden: Ashgate Publishing.

——2006. *Xhosa Beer Drinking Rituals: Power, Practice and Performance in the South African Rural Periphery.* Durham, NC: Carolina Academic Press.

McDonald, M. (ed.) 1994. *Gender, Drink and Drugs.* New York: Berg.

McGovern, P. E. 2003. *Ancient Wine: The Search for the Origins of Viniculture.* Princeton, NJ: Princeton University Press.

——2009. *Uncorking the Past: The Quest for Wine, Beer and Other Alcoholic Beverages.* Berkeley: University of California Press.

McGovern, P. E., S. J. Fleming, and S. Katz. (eds.) 1996. *The Origins and Ancient History of Wine.* Amsterdam: Gordon and Breach Publishers.

McGovern, P. E., E. D. Butrym, A. Nunez, C. S. Wang, M. P. Richards, R. A. Moreau, J. G. Tang, J. Z. Zhang, G. R. Hall, and Z. Q. Zhang. 2004. "Fermented Beverages of Pre- and Proto-Historic China." *Proceedings of the National Academy of Sciences.* November. www.pnas.org cgi/doi/10.1073/pnas.0407921102 (accessed December 16, 2011).

McGrath, A. 1993. "Beneath the Skin: Australian Citizenship, Rights and Aboriginal Women." In R. Howe (ed.) "Women and the State", *Journal of Australian Studies* 37 (June): 99–114.

Mehta, J. N. n. d. *Alcohol and State Revenue.* New Delhi: All India Prohibition Council.

Michalak, L. and K. Trocki. 2006. "Alcohol and Islam: An Overview." *Contemporary Drug Problems* 33 (4) (Winter): 523–62.

Minai, K. 1986. *Trends in Alcoholic Beverage Consumption in Postwar Japan: An Analysis and Interpretation of Aggregate Data.* Singapore: Department of Japanese Studies National University of Singapore.

Moore, J. D. 1989. "Pre-Hispanic Beer in Coastal Peru: Technology and Social Context of Prehistoric Production." *American Anthropologist* 91 (3): 682–95.

O'Brian, J. M. and S. C. Seller. 1982. "Attributes of Alcohol in the Old Testament." *The Drinking and Drug Practices Surveyor* 18: 18–24.

Okrent, D. 2010. *Last Call: The Rise and Fall of Prohibition.* New York: Scribner.

Pan, L. 1975. *Alcohol in Colonial Africa.* Vol. 22. Uppsala: The Scandinavian Institute of African Studies, and Helsinki: The Finnish Foundation for Alcohol Studies.

Paper, J. 1995. *The Spirits are Drunk: Comparative Approaches to Chinese Religion.* Albany: State University of New York Press.

Peele, S. and M. Grant. 1999. *Alcohol and Pleasure: A Health Perspective.* Philadelphia: Brunner/Mazel.

Pernanen, K. 1991. *Alcohol in Human Violence.* New York: The Guilford Press.

Phillips, R. 2000. *A Short History of Wine.* New York: Harper Collins.

Platt, B. 1955. "Some Traditional Alcoholic Beverages and Their Importance in Indigenous African Communities." *Proceedings of the Nutrition Society* 14: 115–24.

Poo, M.-C. 1995. *Wine and Wine Offering in the Religion of Ancient Egypt.* London: Kegan Paul International.

Prakash, O. 1961. *Food and Drinks in Ancient India: From Earliest Times to C. 1200 A.D.* Delhi: Munshi ram Manohar Lal.

Purcell, N. 1985. "Wine and Wealth in Ancient Italy." *The Journal of Roman Studies* 75: 1–19.

Raymond, I. W. 1927. *The Teaching of the Early Church on the Use of Wine and Strong Drink.* New York: Columbia University Press.

Read, B. E. n. d. *Chinese Materia Medica.* Shanghai: Henry Lester Institute for Medical Research.

Roberts, B. D. 2000. "Always Cheaply Pleasant: Beer as Commodity in a Rural Kenyan Society." In A. Haugerud, M. P. Stone, and P. D. Little (eds.) New *Commodities and Globalization, Anthropological Perspectives.* York: Rowman & Littlefield.

Room, R. 1984. "Alcohol and Ethnography: A Case of Problem Deflation?" *Current Anthropology* 25 (2): 169–91.

Rothbaum, N. 2007. *The Business of Spirits: How Savvy Marketers, Innovative Distillers, and Entrepreneurs Changed How We Drink.* New York: Kaplan.

Rumbarger, J. J. 1989. *Profits, Power, and Prohibition: Alcohol Reform and the Industrializing of America, 1800–1930.* Albany, NY: State University of New York Press.

Sadoun, R., G. Lolli, and M. Silverman. 1965. *Drinking in French Culture.* New Brunswick, NJ: Rutgers Center of Alcohol Studies.

Saul, M. 1981. "Beer, Sorghum and Women: Production for the Market in Rural Upper Volta." *Africa* 51 (3): 746–64.

Scardaville, M. C. 1980. "Alcohol Abuse and Tavern Reform in Late Colonial Mexico City." *The Hispanic American Historial Review* 60 (4): 643–71.

Scheidel, W. and S. von Reden. 2002. *The Ancient Economy.* New York: Routledge.

Scholliers, P. (ed.) 2001. *Food, Drink and Identity: Cooking, Eating and Drinking in Europe Since the Middle Ages.* New York: Berg.

Single, E., P. Morgan, and J. de Lint. (eds.) 1981. *Alcohol, Society, and the State: The Social History of Control Policy in Seven Countries.* Toronto: Addition Research Foundation and World Health Organization.

Smith, S. R. 1992. "Drinking Etiquette in a Changing Beverage Market." In J. J. Tobin (ed.) *Re-Made in Japan.* New Haven, CT: Yale University Press.

Snyder, C. R. 1958. *Alcohol and the Jews: A Cultural Study of Drinking and Sobriety.* New Haven, CT: Yale Center of Alcohol Studies.

Ssu-Hsieh, C. (of the later Wei Dynasty) 1945."The Preparation of Ferments and Wines." Trans. H. Tzu-Ch'ing and C. Yünts'ung. *Harvard Journal of Asiatic Studies* 9 (1): 24–44.

Tamang, J. P. 2010. *Himalayan Fermented Foods: Microbiology, Nutrition, and Ethnic Values.* New York: CRC Press, Taylor & Francis Group.

Taylor, W. B. 1979. *Drinking, Homicide, and Rebellion in Colonial Mexican Villages.* Stanford, CA: Stanford University Press.

Valamoti, M. and M. Koukouli-Chrysanthaki. 2007. "Grape-pressings from northern Greece: the earliest wine in the Aegean." *Antiquity* 81 (311): 54–61.

Waltham, C. (ed.) 1971. "Announcement About Drunkenness." In *ShuChing Book of History,* Chicago: Henry Regency Co.

Waltham, C. and Legge, J. 1971. "Announcement About Drunkenness." In *ShuChing Book of History.* Chicago: Henry Regency Co.

Watney, J. 1974. *Beer is Best: A History of Beer.* London: Peter Owen.

White, S. 1996. *Russia Goes Dry: Alcohol, State and Society.* Cambridge: Cambridge University Press.

Wilson, H. 1988. *Egyptian Food and Drink.* Princes Risborough: Shire Publications.

Wolcott, H. F. 1974. *The African Beer Gardens of Bulawayo: Integrated Drinking in a Segregated Society.* New Brunswick, NJ: Rutgers Center of Alcohol Studies.

Zhang, F.-P. 1982. "Drinking in China." *The Drinking and Drug Practices Surveyor* 18: 12–15.

Index

absinthe 66
abuse of alcohol: Australia 94; Britain
65–6; China 108, 109, 110; effects 2,
125; Egypt 12; France 117, 118, 119;
India 92, 106, 107; indigenous Africans
85, 88; indigenous Latin Americans
under Spanish rule 56–9, 62;
industrialization and 78–9; Ireland 67,
68; Japan 112; Jewish society 15, 16;
mortality rates 99; prevention and
treatment 2; Russia 77, 78, 112–15;
Saudi Arabia 104–6; United States 72,
74, 75, 119, 122–3; violence and 101, 125
advertising 71, 98, 120, 134
Africa: alcohol consumption and
production 24, 81–91, 95–6, 131;
alcohol taxation 82, 88, 96, 124, 133;
colonization 81; globalization 101–4;
slave trade 46, 49, 133; South 49–50,
81, 82, 84, 87, 88–9, 133; viticulture
24; West 46, 48–9, 61, 62, 82;
Westernization 124, 130
agriculture 5, 35, 38, 48, 58, 129
aguardiente 57
Akhenaton 10
alcohol: abuse see abuse; academic
disciplines study 1–2; consumption
patterns 14, 33, 44, 58, 63, 95, 124,
130–1; distilled 41; European trade
46; exotic 113, 119, 120, 130; flushing
response 110, 122; globalization and
98–100, 123–5; imperialism and 81;
origins 3, 5–6; poisoning 115; price
14, 42; prohibition see prohibition;
regulation see regulation; ritual
significance 29–30; role in societies 3;
social rituals 20–1; symbolic
meanings 129; taxation see taxation;
what is? 2–3

Alcoholics Anonymous: China 108, 109;
India 106, 107–8; meetings 75; Russia
114; United States 119, 123;
worldwide spread 125
alcoholism: China 18, 110; as a disease
2, 75, 119, 123, 125, 130; Egypt 12;
France 71, 118; Mexico 101; Russia
114–16; Saudi Arabia 105; United
States 122–3
ale 39–44, 50, 53, 55, 130
alehouses 40, 42
Americas, pre-colonial 34–7
America, Latin: alcohol abuse and
temperance movements 125; colonial
regulation of alcohol 58–60, 132;
colonization 46, 54–60, 129–30;
indigenous consumption patterns 54,
57–8, 101; indigenous production
55–6, 131; introduction of distilled
alcohol 54–5; payment in alcohol
133; viticulture 56–7; world
trade 100–1
America, North 46, 50–3
Anatolia 26
Anderson, Kym 98
Angola 49, 83–4, 133
Anstie, Dr. Francis 65
Aristotle 26
arrack 107
Asante 86–7
Australia 81, 93–5, 96, 99, 117, 132
Avicenna 35
Aztecs: medical use of alcohol 44; pulque
consumption patterns 35–6, 44, 57;
regulation of alcohol consumption 35,
36, 44, 54, 57, 130, 132

Babylonia 13–14
baijiu 108

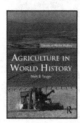

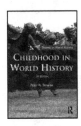

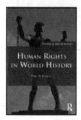

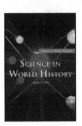

www.tandf.co.uk/journals/RSHI

From Routledge Journals

Social History

Editor: Janet Blackman,
University of Hull, UK

Founding Editor: Keith Nield

**Listed in the Thomson Reuters Arts & Humanities
Citation Index®**

For more than thirty years, *Social History* has published scholarly work of consistently high quality, without restrictions of period or geography. *Social History* is now minded to develop further the scope of the journal in content and to seek further experiment in terms of format. The editorial object remains unchanged - to enable discussion, to provoke argument, and to create space for criticism and scholarship.

In recent years the content of *Social History* has expanded to include a good deal more European and American work as well as, increasingly, work from and about Africa, South Asia and Latin America. In the main, the bulk of this work has taken traditional form - that is, the shape of the scholarly article has determined the form of presentation, its narrative styles and its footnote apparatus. In some circumstances this format can constrain originality, at the worst, or, maybe less bad, it serves to limit conceptual or theoretical risk. We do not wish to argue here that the tradition is without merit. Far from it. Yet we do not judge it appropriate for all purposes. On the contrary, *Social History* will also welcome work which, rather than reproducing past practices, seeks innovation in focus and presentation.

Visit www.tandf.co.uk/journals/RSHI for:
- Online sample copy
- Call for papers
- Instructions for Authors
- Back issues
- Content alerts
- Pricing and Ordering